Living in the Shadow of the Ego

LIVING IN THE SHADOW OF THE EGO

Unraveling the Layers of Self-Identity and Detaching From the Ego to End Suffering

TIM M. HARDTKE

TH

For my readers who finds a piece of themselves within these chapters.

"If you had not suffered as you have, there would be no depth to you as a human being, no humility, no compassion. You would not be reading this now. Suffering cracks open the shell of ego, and then comes a point when it has served its purpose. Suffering is necessary until you realize it is unnecessary."

— Eckhart Tolle, *Stillness Speaks*

Contents

Author's Note

The More Present You Live, the Less Suffering You Will Experience in Life!

Chapter 1

THE SPIRITUAL SEARCH

THE SPIRITUAL SEARCH or even the search for the meaning of life often begins for many reasons, such as when something tragic happens to yourself or your loved ones, or when questions begin to arise time and time again in your life after you realize that you have no control over anything. Questions such as, "Why does life have to be this way? Why is it so difficult? Where do I fit in? What is my calling? Why do bad things happen to good people? Why is there so much suffering? Why are all these things happening over and over when I don't want them to?" These questions lead to the beginning of self-awareness arising in the present moment because the strong attachment to the ego-self is slowly releasing. This releasing mental attachment produces the doorway for the illusion of the ego to be left behind and the presence of self-awareness to emerge. It is kind of like saying out of the darkness of unawareness and into the light of self-awareness.

The ego illusions can weigh you down so heavily that you just can't go on another year, another day, or even another moment living like this. You know something better is out there waiting for you, but you just don't know what it is or how to attain it. A lot of times you look around at others and you want what they have, but ultimately in most cases what they have are more egoic illusions taking on a different form. You could say it's the same suffering only it looks more desirable.

The opposite could be true at the same time, where you believed you knew exactly who you were, and you had a razor-sharp focus on a single goal. You could have spent many years of your life chasing after this goal to become the person you saw yourself as, and once you achieved it, self-awareness was once again allowed to enter the present moment and for the first time in a long time you were able to take a step back and look at your life and felt a bit lost and thought to yourself, "Now what?"

For me, it happened when I felt so lost. I felt like I didn't know who I was or what I was supposed to be. I could see what the world and others wanted me to be, but I just couldn't agree with that. It just didn't feel right living so deeply depending on the world of form to survive or to tell me who I was. I didn't see life working forty hours a week for forty years of my life, all the while trying to live life between all that. The question kept constantly arising, "Why does this always depend on *that*? Why was I born into a world where I automatically have to do something to survive? Why is there so much doing and never any being? Why do we have to constantly do the same things daily to keep up one big illusion that we are successful in life?"

The thought of having a regular job or a regular life was never the problem, but the same emptiness of just passing time day after day getting from this form just to go home to experience that form felt wrong and selfish. Looking back, I could see the Yo-Yo effect on my life and the different extremes I was bouncing back and forth from helping others tremendously one year and feeling good about myself to being selfish and not helping hardly anybody in the next year, which made me depressed. Then I would go from outgoing and fun to reclusive and just wanting to be left alone. I would hide, play video games, or read books. I would do things that can be done alone and don't require anybody else to experience. I was using a mental/emotional/physical (this) to produce a mental/emotional/physical (that) experience.

I was so heavily stuck in the ego experience that I knew something was wrong and there had to be a better way to live, but I just accepted it as life kicking me in the ass, over and over, and believing that if I didn't play along, I would not survive. Looking back, I realize that good or bad, life is primarily lived in the mind if you are not present enough to experience it as it is happening. The movement of going back and forth between mental, physical, and emotional extremes was taking its toll on me, yet I didn't seem to have any control to stop it. I would look back and think to myself, "Why did I have to say or do such things in the heat of the moment?" I came to find out the answer was simple; my ego-self was completely dominating my awareness at the moment I was saying or doing things that I didn't want to, yet the reaction time between words or actions was so quick and programmed that true self-awareness never once had an opportunity to arise. In essence, I was just acting out the character and storyline of "Tim," as if it was absolutely real and happening to this shrunken little ego-self that was created in my mind based on the total of all past experiences. This little shrunken ego-self needed constant defense to maintain its solidity in my mind. The importance of getting things perfect or winning every moment of every day was my ego being in control and having to defend my beliefs. It was the very cause of my suffering. We all know that if you don't win, even if it is just an argument, suffering arises. The ego always tries to be perceived as positive, yet at the same time, it always wants to get its way, which is selfish and therefore a negative experience.

The ego illusion itself is so seductive that I would constantly be aware of all these negative thoughts and emotions that are simply not there when you are self-aware or fully present. Self-awareness completely obliterates the negative thoughts and emotions that are constantly arising in the mind/body experience. I don't even notice them anymore when I'm self-aware or living in the fully present moment, as I am no longer judging every single thing that arises. I am learning to fully accept things without the need to instantly change them for what I consider to be better. My entire life experience is more about witnessing thoughts of consciousness, the present moment, and wanting to help others gain a better understanding of both, knowing that there is also an opposite to that awareness that is present at the same time as well, meaning I still witness egoic thoughts, but now I know the difference. I know that if I fail miserably and don't help anybody, having an awareness of the present moment is the only success that we all need when searching for our true identity. As the spiritual search continues, we begin to have choices when none were present before. The more we try new ways of doing things, the more spaciousness we have for the allowance of form to arise without experiencing suffering, even when it is less than favorable for ourselves.

All the things that are arising in your daily life in the form of outward experiences now have the possibility of having options, or what you might call the dissolution of absolutes.

You can choose at each moment exactly what form you want to experience in your life, instead of only seeing one absolute way to do things.

The ego experience itself is like a freight train; it stops for nobody. Either your conscious awareness is completely dominated by it, or you have awareness of it at which point you would probably not need a book of this nature as you would already experience this type of awareness. The egoic experience has set patterns based on old habits, and when these old habits are witnessed in the mind, it just carries itself out with zero thought given to any action. It is like picking up and lighting your next cigarette. You give zero awareness to it consciously as it just happens all on its own, based on mental attachments to past habits. Let's face it, if we were all fully aware of every single time, we harmed ourselves or others in one manner or another, we would always choose not to, wouldn't we? Living in the ego experience is what has taken that ability away from us, by covering up the present moment with more of our individual dramatic and selfish storylines.

Self-awareness on the other hand, which is hopefully what you find by giving up the need to search for spiritual knowledge, will bring your full attention back to the present moment as you start to look at every single action and reaction at every second of the day. If you practice doing that then self-awareness will allow you to choose whether in this moment you want to smoke, or you want to overeat, or you want to do drugs, etc. as nothing is set in stone and everything in the ego experience is a choice. There is no egoic desire arising that you instinctively react to, or a constant pull witnessed that almost forces you to light the next cigarette. There is only peace and awareness. It is completely effortless to choose not to smoke; because your conscious awareness is not fully focused on a mind-dominated egoic state, as you are fully in the moment or in a formless state of being when you experience the freedom of the present moment! If you choose, you can be a silent witness as the world of form is happening all around you.

This is the difference between letting the ego illusion dominate your entire life with no control over it, or being fully self-aware enough to experience the present moment of your life exactly the way you want in total control and having full awareness of this experience. In the end, the spiritual search is often a shift from the denial of the present moment, towards the full acceptance of the present moment. The more you understand the illusion of the ego, the less suffering is witnessed and the deeper connection to consciousness will be experienced.

Chapter 2

MY STORYLINE

*Warning: this chapter was written before I became aware of the conscious-
ness that we all work from, but I'm not changing it to leave it as another
pointer to the mind-dominated state of consciousness! It points to how caught
up in the form of spirituality I was at the time and still completely lost in the
ego searching for myself until the moment that self-realization happened.
More than likely, it will be the easiest chapter in this book to fully understand
as it is filled with mind-dominated concepts and points of view.*

THE EGO NEEDS a storyline so here is mine. My spiritual search began in
July 2004, after I met a guy named Kosol. My friend Jake who worked
with him had been telling me all the stories about how he could read
anybody's aura in the entire world without ever meeting them or seeing
them, and he wanted to introduce me to him.

We went to his house where he was teaching a meditation class at
that time, so we sat on the couch with all the other people who were
waiting to meditate in the back room. After twenty minutes or so had
gone by, five or six people came out of the back bedroom after they had
finished meditating. One of the men was a Cambodian gentleman, who
came over to the couch. My buddy Jake introduced me to him, and he
asked if he could see my aura. Kosol said, "Oh yes" and began

explaining the colors and telling me things about myself and my nature and why I was the way I was and even all these things about me that I've never told anybody, and he continued for about a good ten or twenty minutes.

After he finished, I think I was practically in shock. I couldn't believe how someone I never met could know so much specific details about my life. Then the other people on the couch asked if he could see theirs and he went down the line and read every single person's aura to them the same way he did mine to the point where one of the men started crying because he was touched so deeply. It was amazing to witness such a thing when I never believed up to that point that it was even possible to know people without having physical contact in some way, shape, or form with them.

I was a normal twenty-six-year-old brought up in the Western culture and technology-based environment, who liked to go out with my friends and have fun. I had the 40/40 plan set in my mind, where the only way to make it in life was to work forty hours a week for forty years of my life, maybe get married and have some kids, and then hit retirement and then call it a life.

Up to that point, I was brought up in the Christian church with only a religious background to work from, so I had no context to put this aura reading experience. It was new to me, and I was very intrigued by how this was possible, and I wanted to know more. At this point, that same day after Kosol was done with all the aura readings, I asked him if he could teach me how to do aura readings and he said, "Yes, all you needed to do was learn meditation because aura reading is just a natural side effect of raising your vibrations from meditation." He agreed to teach me his stargate meditation.

I came back the next week to his house and there was a house full of people who were all taking his meditation class then. So, I sat on his couch expecting him to start teaching me something, and the very first thing he said when my meditation lesson began was, "I'm not going to tell you anything; instead, I'm simply going to show you everything based on your own experiences."

He took me into the back room with some of his other students and we all began to meditate together. At first, I remember the room was completely dark and silent. You could only hear the other people breathing. I remember my experiences in the beginning were very simple experiences of just seeing white light coming out of the darkness and at some point, even a light so bright I thought someone was holding a flashlight to my eyes.

The meditation experiences from there began to slowly grow to where I was starting to feel physical sensations in my body, like tingling or experiencing chills, to an extreme level that sustained itself for the entire time of the meditation session. I didn't know it at the time, but I was slowly becoming aware of the energetic vibrations that arise during meditation. I was also becoming aware of the effects when you raise your vibrations to higher dimensions or levels. Time is experienced completely differently in those states of consciousness.

As I advanced in the meditation or to put it differently, my conscious awareness was growing, I began to experience higher levels of consciousness where I thought I only spent a few minutes meditating when I realized two hours had passed here in the physical when I came out of the meditative state. Another natural side effect of my meditations, when I advanced enough, was that I was becoming aware that all I was doing was shifting my consciousness from the world of form to the formless, but out of the formless came the world of form again. This concept of starting at one place, which we call the physical, and then going the distance all the way to the other place, which we call spiritual, was just bringing me back to a physical awareness or the awareness of form itself.

For instance, one time, I started my meditation. I shifted my consciousness from this physical body into the formless, then all of a sudden out of the formless rushed this portal of light and it rushed towards me till all of a sudden, I was witnessing the great pyramids of Egypt being built. I used my eyes to look around in perfect detail, I saw an incredible number of Egyptians building a pyramid. There were a ton of thin cloth-type tents all over the place and the sphinx looked brand new and even had red and green paint on the headdress. It was an amazing experience and just as fast as the awareness arose; I zoomed back out and back into the awareness of this body. I've had tons of those remote viewing experiences, and who knows if it was from this time/space reality or another. It's just another wonderful side effect of meditation.

After the first year of meditating with Kosol, out of the house full of students, my buddy Jake and I were the only ones left. Everyone else realized meditation takes work, and it takes time. They must have not been willing to put in either and slowly gravitated back to their usual activities.

It took about a year to graduate from Kosol's meditation class. I was able to shift my consciousness instantly without using the mechanics of the meditation anymore, and he said I no longer needed the meditation. I was meditating up to five hours a day at one point and I was experiencing levitation in my hands and arms, and they would just float up in the air for thirty minutes or an hour and just hover there. To me, it felt like a huge energy glove around my hands, but I couldn't feel the heaviness from them anymore and my focus was still searching myself out in the formless because I thought my true self was out there in the void somewhere.

Another natural thing that began to happen after the first year that let me know I wasn't this body was instantly when I would shift my consciousness, the body would shut down and instantly begin to snore like it was in sleep mode, yet I was fully conscious and witnessing the body snoring. It was the strangest thing for a while, but even that became normal the more I meditated.

As you can see, my spiritual path has a progression to it, just as all things in this mind/body experience do. My spiritual storyline is being built slowly based on all these experiences I had been having and my mind and ego had slowly shifted gears from I'm just a regular guy to I'm a spiritual seeker.

At this point, I dove into the deep end of the spiritual pool, and I was in search of myself. I read every single spiritual book I could get my hands on; I watched every movie, and I downloaded every clip of spiritual teaching I could find. I did everything I could do in my spare time to be spiritual. I created a meditation area, and I had waterfalls and peaceful pictures on the walls. I had incense and sage. My ego tried to create a spiritual environment to support my spiritual growth.

I began to study spiritual healing and became a Reiki Master. I started working with people teaching them healing and meditation. I was going around online bringing awareness to people who were suffering from a lack of awareness in simple everyday situations by talking to them and helping them raise their consciousness by bringing spiritual knowledge to them.

I was able to read people's auras to them and I just had this knowingness that arose with this deep sense of compassion for them, and it was so easy to read that feeling or that energy when it happened.

At this point I thought to myself, this is it, I'm spiritual, this is what it's like to be spiritual. I had a huge library of books I'd read. I had tons of movies, audiobooks, e-books, and all kinds of spiritual material. I had meditation CDs and was going to spiritual expos at the time. I was seeking this spiritual knowledge so bad that my local library system in my county ran out of spiritual books for me to read so I was once again buying them online and having them shipped to me.

At this point the outward spirituality was being experienced, because I was clinging to the concept or idea of spirituality itself and what it meant to me to be spiritual, and I had this huge collection of spiritual material to back up my beliefs.

All the while I still didn't know who I was or what I was. The years went by, and my life was still happening around me, but almost all day long I was lost in thought dwelling on the nature of the ego and what I thought the ego was. I could see people working from it everywhere all day long and suffering because of it accordingly.

I think at this point I had a very shrunken sense of what the ego was. I had worked past the ego being arrogant and was starting to see it as being the opposite of the spiritual self. When someone was rude or lacked compassion for others, I called that ego. When I saw someone practicing patience or love or opening a door for others, I called that working from their higher self or spiritual self. I was beginning to see it wasn't a matter of doing good or being bad; it was instead an awareness of why we react to certain thoughts the way we do and how these reactions dictate the reality we create in our minds.

I had created a world of opposing concepts that fit neatly in my concept of spirituality and was mentally labeling people spiritual or not spiritual accordingly, thinking to myself, that person doesn't know themselves very well, or wow, that person is very enlightened and balanced. I was reading books about the Buddha at this time, and I was practicing the middle path, and paying close attention to the eight-fold path. All the books on Buddhism pointed to this eight-fold path. I had read about it several times, but I just looked at it and filed it away as I was still on the hunt for the next piece of knowledge.

When I practiced not going to any extreme in my thinking, I started using the eight-fold path fully. This was the beginning of a major shift of consciousness for me.

I started very carefully watching all the things that constantly arose in my mind and was filtering them through the eight-fold path before they came out of my mouth when dealing with people and found myself backtracking my thoughts and actions constantly because my ego-self wanted to be saying and thinking things differently. I was just very carefully beginning to pay close attention to the present moment.

It might not be known to the closest people around me because my ego-self was still playing a role for them that they understood, but my consciousness was focused on something different all the time. I noticed a lot of my friends gravitated away from me and some of them started thinking I was weird, because of the things I was talking about and the experiences I was having in meditation.

My mentor, Kosol, to this day, has never really sat me down and told me anything about spirituality. We talked about common experiences we've both shared, and he's helped guide me along the way based on his own experiences, but it was never like going to school and taking a class. He never once said this is how it is, and you will learn this and pulled out a book and started teaching concepts. He very simply taught me the mechanics of the Stargate method of meditation and healing and let the rest unfold naturally on its own.

It's been five years since I started meditating. I've searched every piece of spiritual knowledge people have left behind in books and whatnot and after all the searching and slowly running out of new material. People constantly recommend books or ads online and say if you like this person, then check out this person. I didn't know what to do next as I just didn't feel complete, and I still wanted to know what the next person that I was exposed to knew. It got to the point where I was picking up new books and reading them thinking, "I know this already" or "this is beginner stuff," because I already had all of those same experiences to work from that people were writing about.

I remember throughout the entire spiritual journey, I would have these huge growth spurts and then I would level off for a while, and then all of a sudden, another huge surge of growth and spiritual experiences to work from. All the time towards the end I was experiencing these huge leaps in consciousness, and it was happening when I was reading a book or writing a blog or just dwelling on the nature of things, and all of a sudden this huge rush of energy would surround my head and I would have this huge epiphany or realization about the nature of things, and in that instant, it seemed like everything was known and I was like AH HAH, and I was able to touch the present moment very deeply.

Like all things in the mind/body experience, just as it arose for me, the feeling and all the knowingness slowly subsided and I was back in the flow of the mind/body experience. I remember this happening several times when I had a major awakening and I would call my mentor and tell him what happened and how I knew this and this and that, and he would always say that's great and explain that my consciousness just experienced a big growth, but you are not quite there yet. Even after all of these things I still didn't feel like I knew who or what I was.

It was just knowing about the nature of the mind/body experience that was exposing itself to me and after the last couple of big realizations, I slowly began to pay close attention to all the things I was not. I started witnessing emotions arise and subside all their own without any effort on my part. I began witnessing the mind and all the thoughts arising and subsiding all on their own and the same with actions from the body. I was taking on a third-person, witnessing role of all these major things that I used to associate myself with. I noticed my consciousness having a dialog with itself at the same time the mind was busy doing its thing on its own. It was getting to the point where I was driving my car and I was witnessing thoughts arising in the mind, and then the body reacting from those thoughts. I witnessed the mind thinking I'm bored, and the body would naturally react by changing the radio station trying to create more atmosphere to keep the mind busy.

At this point, my girlfriend, Heideh, bought me several spiritual books for Valentine's Day, so I switched gears and started reading books by Thich Nhat Hahn. I had read several books on Zen before, but I enjoyed how Thich Nhat Hahn was able to explain the present moment very deeply. I once again tried to find his books at my local library, but out of over 100 publications he's put out, they only had maybe four or five. At this point, I was happy to find something new to read about. It was a book on how to touch the present moment deeply. I thought this was a great concept to research since I had already been touching the moment deeply but didn't realize it.

I also came across a book about Nisagardatta Maharaj called The Ultimate Medicine: *Dialogs with a Realized Master*. My spiritual search up to that point had all been pointing to material about Jesus, Buddha, Krishna, Wayne Dyer, Eckhart Tolle, Deepak Chopra, or Thich Nhat Hahn. Now, I was being pointed to Nisagardatta Maharaj.

I read the book about Nisagardatta, and none of it made any sense to me. I kept thinking, "Wow, this is so deep. I don't understand it." So, I put it on my bookshelf where it sat for a few years. I knew eventually just like with all the other books I had read. Once I had more experiences of the same type of nature, working from the material would begin to fully make sense.

This type of spiritual search just continued.

I was researching spiritual material; I was trying to implement all of it, and I was meditating daily. After all of this effort and progression, I was still only aware that I was neither the mind nor the body but still didn't know what I was. All kinds of outward experiences were happening to me, and I wasn't reacting to them like I had in the past. I had several people close to me die and at first it hurt tremendously, but I kind of got over it pretty quickly. I knew I wasn't just this body or this mind, and I knew they weren't those things either. I could see that the only thing that happened was their consciousness shifted to something else, and this physical experience no longer served them a purpose.

To those around me at the time, it seemed heartless not to grieve for an extended period, but I was no longer clinging to the ego illusion or false sense of self. I noticed all the things that used to make me so angry in the past didn't even get a reaction from me anymore. I witnessed anger arising in my mind. I could see that my ego-self was feeling attacked and wanted to retaliate with anger, yet I was no longer clinging to the mind like that anymore. As I witnessed this anger arising in the mind and I didn't react by clinging to it like the mind was ME, I then saw the anger subside and the mind would become calm again like nothing happened, even if someone was yelling at me.

This happened again over two days after getting into an argument with my girlfriend over something silly, I witnessed my ego-self fully reacting to her ego-self, and I saw the two egos going back and forth, yet "I" in the deepest sense, wasn't a part of the argument. The same thing happened the next day. I saw my ego-self react to her ego-self, and the dialog was going back and forth, and I was on the inside screaming no, I don't want to say those things, no, I don't mean that, what is going on?

The argument continued until she and my friend Jeff got out of my car to go have lunch, but I told them I was going to stay in the car. At this point, it was April 4, 2009. I was thirty-one years old and outwardly I was sitting in my car alone in a parking lot, having just been in an argument with my girlfriend, and then it happened. As I sat alone in silence, dwelling on what just happened and how was this possible, I realized that I had no control over the mind/body anymore. Thoughts arose about how this could happen. What just happened? What was this huge space between what I thought was me, and this peaceful void that was like nothingness?

Chapter 3

THE AWAKENING

I AM GOING to speak quickly about the awakening experience as it happened to me. I have yet to find anybody talking about what exactly happened to him or her other than saying it happened when they were gardening or doing the dishes or mowing the lawn when they became "awakened," or aware of the present moment, so I thought I would share. Don't get caught up in the form it took for me, as I'm sure it could be completely different for others, but ultimately the awareness will be the same. When it happens, there is no mistaking what has happened. Not even Jesus himself could convince you otherwise. It leaves zero room for error, as it is not experienced in the mind.

As I was sitting in my car alone contemplating the awareness of the rising of separation that occurred between the illusion of the ego and the present moment, suddenly everything went completely black. I turned inward and witnessed a zooming-out effect from everything I was looking at, all the way to total darkness. The awareness of the body and the mind completely disappeared. It was like zooming out from the location of my car to the state I was in, then above the earth, then beyond the universe. At the same time, I could see my entire life unfolding instantly like a deck of cards being shuffled face up.

I witnessed all the major events that occurred over my entire life that led me to believe who I thought I was and also what I thought I was. I witnessed the ego unfolding itself completely. The biggest illusion of all was finally seen for what it was and, in an instant, the only thing that was left after I deeply touched the present moment was consciousness itself or the formless awareness.

I could see how everything in the mind/body experience was a concept. I saw my entire life and the very thought of the egoic me was one concept based on another concept, etc. I could see how everything contained in the mind existed in the awareness of the mind/body experience only. That everything in the mind/body experience was based on opposing forces or opposites. I could also see that consciousness itself is the only thing that has no opposite because it is not based on the world of form or even dependent on the world of form. Consciousness is in fact what makes the world of form even possible and also what makes all things possible for without awareness of consciousness anything contained in the world of form would not have a place to arise and subside from or even a reason to arise or in the first place.

I also witnessed the conceptualized story of Adam and Eve quickly play out. We all existed as pure consciousness before the fruit was eaten from the tree of knowledge, meaning pure consciousness or full presence is our natural state of being.

After the fruit was eaten, the world of form was born, and they instantly realized they were naked. I didn't witness an actual event; I witnessed the concept behind the story unfolding. This is where my awareness of form comes from. I also saw something about Buddha and Nirvana, but I don't remember exactly what it was. The point is that it was another pointer to the truth of what we are that can't possibly be explained to another. It has to be experienced firsthand.

Just when you think you have life or spirituality or religion figured out in your mind and you feel extremely secure in it you don't, as you only have that particular form figured out and this truth will be known the moment that particular form is challenged or taken away completely. Just when you think you've read enough books to have a perfect understanding of the information or teaching, you don't, you only have a perfect understanding of the form or mental concepts the writer was expressing. Just when you think thirty years of meditation in a cave locked away from the world makes you enlightened, it doesn't. True peacefulness and awareness can only be found in the present moment where you are free from all human suffering no matter what is happening to you or around you.

Ultimately, no amount of knowledge, no set amount of meditation, no amount of anything that has form can let you know what you truly are. You must be willing to give it all up to be present enough to experience self-awareness for yourself. You can only find what you are searching for in the present moment. It can't be found in thirty years of spiritual research and retreats taken all around the world. That only leads to a strengthening of the ego. Just because you took lessons from an enlightened master and think that means something, it doesn't, as you are already an enlightened master yourself. You simply haven't given up the world of form to touch the formless yet, which is why the majority of all teachers in the world are only able to teach the form that was taught to them and nothing more.

The only thing you need to do to experience true self-awareness is to work at being fully present. To create an opening in the present moment that will allow the awakening process to happen for you. It doesn't cost any money; it doesn't require ownership of spiritual items or belongings. It only requires a willingness on your part to touch the present moment deeper than you ever have before. It's not found by searching for it, it is found by the willingness to give everything of form up for your awareness to return to it. The division between the illusion of the ego and the core of your being can only be seen in this moment right now. At this very moment, you already are the very thing you are searching for; you simply aren't aware of it. Yet, because you are busy searching for yourself in the world of form, you are looking to your past to tell you who you are, or you are busy working extremely hard to build a future to tell you who you are going to be. If you are busy trying to find your place in the world, that pointer alone will tell you that you are stuck searching in the world of form. The focus of your life at this moment in time will let you know what form you are searching for yourself in. If you are busy trying to maintain a marriage or a relationship, then that is a form. If you are constantly trying to increase your wealth, then that is a form. If you have given most of the usual forms up that everyone loses themselves in and starts a spiritual search, then that also has a form, and you could easily get caught up in that.

If you are busy wondering who you are or searching for who you are or doing those types of things, then how could you possibly be present enough to touch consciousness, as it exists formless right now in the present moment? How can you experience the core of your being if you are busy chasing illusions in your mind? You can try a million different ways to find yourself, but if you're not doing it in the present moment, then in the end, it's just going to be the same thing, taking on a million different forms.

After deeply touching the present moment that day in my car, I remember re-reading all the books that never made sense to me. When I picked up the first book about Nisagardatta Maharaj, it shockingly made perfect sense to me. I read the Bible again, and it was the same thing. It was full of pointers to that state of consciousness, only using things of form like stories and metaphors to point. Once I gave up clinging to the literal interpretation that is experienced in the mind, I was able to see all the wonderful pointers that other religious and spiritual teachers had left behind. We live in a world full to the brim with pointers; the only problem is we are using the context of our ego-self to attempt to filter those pointers through the mind to rationalize them out into a literal context that does not work.

When a spiritual teacher somewhere says that a bird and a river are the same thing, the mind gets lost trying to rationalize how a bird and a river can be the same thing, because it attempts to use a literal interpretation.

I knew after seeing pointers in everything that I had an awakening experience, and I now had the proper context to put the entire content of the world into. The feeling of peace and freedom was so amazing that when Heideh and Jeff got back into my car, I had the biggest smile on my face from feeling a tremendous and overwhelming sense of beingness or presence. I guess maybe I was truly high on life for the first time.

The last thing I'll share about this experience is the understanding that things of form are all the same things. I gave the example of a bird and a river, but form is form. Ultimately, this book is no different from a computer, your body, or a tree, and at the same time, this thought is no different from that thought, etc. In the mind/body experience, they all have a form or a shape or a color or a difference of some kind, but to consciousness, they are all the same thing, form itself! The consciousness that is at the core of your being is only a spectator to the world of form. The majority of your entire life is spent witnessing thought forms, let alone the body or all of the other forms that exist outwardly in the world. Form is what dominates the mind/body experience.

The ego experiences the doing-ness of thought forms that are reacted to which, in turn, can cause suffering, but the majority of your happiness will stem from the times you will experience stillness in all non-reaction. Stillness is one of the best pointers you can find in abundance in the mind/body experience. You will see that a book that is not opened by you just sits there, a computer not used by you just sits there, or a car not used by you just sits there in stillness. It is only when we use each form for its intended conceptualized purpose that we lose the ability to point to the present moment and begin to serve the ego once again. You will see that it is humans that are constantly moving the world; without humans on earth, would there still be a motion to all these forms? Does a car have consciousness enough to want to drive itself down a road? I'm sure some people define themselves by trying to progress technology to the point where this is a reality, but what good would a car that drives itself down a road be today if there were still people who are starving to death somewhere in the world?

Why is chasing mind movements more important than helping all others achieve the necessities to just simply exist without a daily fight to stay alive? Would there still be a need for the ego to continue using things of form to define itself if we shifted our perspective from progressing as individuals to learning how to progress as a whole? These simple questions have a form to them, and it is the ego that labels them good questions to ask or bad ones as there are as many questions one could ask as there are thoughts in the mind. Learning to see the world of form from the viewpoint of self-awareness is a necessary context to have to help shed the individuality that exists in the ego, which causes separation from all others.

In the mind-dominated ego state of consciousness, this book is different from a computer or your body, but to see differences everywhere you look is ultimately what keeps you stuck in the ego and also what keeps mankind separate from one another. When separation occurs, so does suffering. The proper understanding of true self-realization is needed to see six billion people as the same thing you are, only taking on six billion different forms. Jesus said to love thy neighbor as thyself, and an understanding from that pointer comes only after you have the proper context to hold that teaching in. In the context of the mind, to see another as yourself might mean to see another human. But to only see the concept of a human is to leave that interpretation wide open to all things that exist in the mind. One person sees a conceptualized human as one thing, while the next sees it completely differently, as it depends on the individualized ego. In the context of full self-awareness or consciousness, to see another is simply to see the consciousness that is behind the outward form their ego has taken. It exists perfectly and completely as it does not require a definition to exist, nor can any label truly define it. Awakening to the consciousness within is the only way to truly understand it as the form to communicate it by calling it consciousness does not truly do it justice at all. The communicated form only leaves it floating around in the mind as another concept, but it is the most beautiful thing to have an awareness of and the only thing I know of that is truly eternal and the greatest thing about it is it is already who you are at this very moment! You can attempt to separate yourself from the thought of it, but it is the one thing that has never left and will never leave you. The peace that you are as it exists in the present moment is the only thing you will ever or can ever truly be. You can throw a tantrum like a child and attempt to prove that statement wrong by causing suffering to yourself or others, but suffering is not eternal and therefore a completely meaningless hobby of the ego.

Ultimately, my spiritual search has ended. There is nothing left to search for. Everything is found at this very second right here in the present moment, and all I want to do is help others find the end to their suffering as well. For me, the cycle of uncontrollable suffering has ended, and now I have a chance to truly live a life as it is intended to be lived—in the present moment. The differences I notice now are the lack of desire to live a huge, amazing life full of the most pleasant and wonderful things. I don't want to know everything about everything anymore. I don't want to keep up illusions with other people to make me feel secure or feel like I am somebody. The less I remain lost in deep thought about something, the more present, and the less ambitious I am, the more present I stay. Ambition to the mind is a good thing. Losing yourself in the form that ambition takes is something completely different. The sense of doing something or needing something or having something or wanting to know something only exists in the ego experience—which is void of the present moment as the ego requires the next thing. The next step, and the next piece of knowledge or discovery, is why the ego has a constant motion to it. Ultimately, you need to stop the motion to find yourself to stop all suffering. You need to jump off the moving train and land with both feet securely in the present moment. If you can remain present, then when the time comes, if you are ever called to help others, you will have nothing standing in your way, no matter how big or how small the task is. The selfishness of the ego will have diminished, and the peace and willingness of the present moment will be all that is needed to face new opportunities in life with an open mind and an open heart.

Chapter 4

A WARENESS OF CONSCIOUSNESS

To start, consciousness gives you the ability to witness a couple of the biggest things that our ego is derived from. First, is the mind. Second, is the body. When you bring the two types of awareness together, you get the mind/body experience. The mind is what the majority of all human beings are stuck witnessing because it is in a constant state of motion, which is what I call the mind-dominated state of consciousness. There is no space or stillness available to see it for what it truly is because unless you are firmly rooted in the present moment, it simply never stops. The first problem with the awareness of the mind-dominated state of consciousness as being your only source of information about who you are to pull from is that the mind is in a constant state of reaction. There is no stillness to the mind. You need to ask yourself how you can know who you truly are when you are constantly reacting to everything around you and allowing those reactions to express who you think you are. The instant reaction of the mind does not allow you to react as you truly want to react; instead, you simply end up reacting how you have been programmed to react over the years in defense of an ego-self. The next biggest problem with only having the awareness of the mind-dominated state is that everything contained in the mind is a concept and the only difference between this concept or that concept ultimately is the context in which it is held, which once again continues to form the ego based on which concepts you hold near and dear to your heart. This is why the ego fights for survival when any of the concepts that you hold to be absolute truth are challenged.

What is consciousness in the first place? What is this thought of "I" or this thought of "me" or self or whatever label is placed on it? For most people, consciousness itself is simply just the awareness of form, such as thoughts or emotions or all the senses of the body. For others who have become what people call fully conscious, it is an awareness in its purest form meaning the awareness that form and the formless can exist at the same time. The mind is only aware of form itself, whereas full consciousness is aware of the formless or the nothingness that exists in the present moment at the same time that the mind is still being witnessed. Full consciousness is being aware of both extremes of consciousness at the same time. It is an awareness that ultimately there is absolute stillness and peace present even amidst the most horrific outward experiences.

Let's use a metaphor for consciousness and call it life.

At the beginning of life, you are a baby. You can consider this to be the state of full self-realization. There is nothing added to it. Nothing can be taken away; there is no concept of time. You haven't even been told yet that you are a human; you just know that you exist without the need to add anything, as you exist purely in the moment. A baby is not even witnessing their mind as what is there of form yet that has accumulated other than "I exist." Have you ever heard of a baby being born and instantly saying, "Give me a cigarette?" Of course, not as your ego needs time to begin collecting forms such as food and warmth or any outward desires or even the love of its parents. Now, as you begin to grow up, the awareness of consciousness or the thought "I exist" is being force-fed all kinds of other things that slowly begin to wash away that pure state of awareness.

As the mind begins to accumulate its definitions of what is being witnessed, things like the concept of speech are witnessed, the concept of body and movement is witnessed, the concept of clothes, and an infinite number of things start to cover up the pure self-awareness of "I exist" with all the things that come from the five senses. All kinds of forms are being witnessed with the eyes, the ears, the nose, the mouth, the body in general, etc. Eventually, you are taught that these forms have names, even your body has a name. You will, from this day forward, be known as "Timothy." Think about that for a second, as this is where all individuality stems from. Without the form of a body being named Timothy, would the world consider each egoic attachment that makes up my personality? Would the world consider my particular sense of humor, Timothy? Everything that makes up the concept of a person is stuffed inside a body by individualizing certain concepts and giving them ownership based on the arising of a human body. If this body were to subside, would you see humor arising in another and instantly call that Timothy?

As the world of form begins to unfold for you, it is with the help of others that you are taught these individual forms have a color; they have a taste; they have a smell; they have a feeling to them. You are even taught they all have a purpose. You are taught that all things of form exist to serve you like clothes, a car, food, a toothbrush, a television, a computer, books, an education, religion, money, and the concept of a job. Even in some cases, you might be taught that other people exist to service you as well. This is where the thought of me or mine begins to develop. The great division or separation from others begins to occur as well. As you continue to cling to the ideas of what others who have come before you are teaching you, you begin to develop this false sense of self. The purest form of consciousness now has a label—it now has a family.

Eventually, it will have friends, and it will know sickness and diseases, birth and death, mental and emotional problems, and someday it might own a house and car and maybe have kids. There are no limits to how far this illusory self or what I call the ego can be witnessed. This is the true experience of the mind/body ego-self and the birth of all human suffering. When you reach adulthood, this sense of self has over time developed its personality based on all the concepts that are clung to in the mind and that is all based on the experiences of the five senses, and the concept of the past, or what the illusory self has thought it experienced, led you to believe that it is all real and has meant something. This is where the concept of the thought, "Well, it happened to me, so I know it's real" is born. The ego begins to take ownership over certain experiences that people define themselves by because of the belief that they are that way because it happened to them. The ego isn't in the business of letting go of anything of form; it has all added up to who you believe yourself to be at this moment. As life continues to progress, so does this division between the awareness of your consciousness that needs to retain nothing and the awareness of your ego that needs to retain everything. The ego draws a line in the sand and says if you have nothing to show for all of your years on earth, then you are nothing. This is why the major pursuit in life is that of some form of outward success or the acquisition of material belongings. If you were to do the math, you would see that very few people spend their lives in service to others while the rest, knowingly or unknowingly, seek to benefit from others.

The process of releasing egoic attachments is the process of returning your conscious awareness from the heavy world of mental form and back to your natural formless state or effortless state of being. You will see that the only differences in the levels of consciousness are simply the various levels of self-realization by egoic release. The more you look for the formlessness of consciousness, the more self-awareness will become present in your immediate awareness, no matter what the circumstances.

Self-awareness is not a knowledge-based scale, because all knowledge is mental form added up to create a concept. If one person has huge knowledge about one single conceptualized form, such as spirituality or religion, then the ego can misuse that form, which in turn can cause separation from all others who do not live their life by the same concepts. This is why it is so important to see the formless consciousness that we all stem from to see everybody as the same in different forms.

Chapter 5

THE MIND

I DESCRIBE the mind as a place where all concepts gained throughout your entire life are stored. It is a warehouse full of knowledge that is gained outwardly, and it is also the area of your awareness that makes all things possible, and all seem real. Within the mind exists the suffering of all mankind, heaven and hell, aliens, and the belief that the human body is you. Absolutely anything that a person has ever thought up or could dream of exists in the mind.

The mind is where imagination and desires manifest as form. A small part of consciousness is given an incredibly huge playing field. Your conscious awareness is now focused on mental form, and those mental forms consist of concepts built on other concepts and considered to be real. It is these few simple truths that make the mind the birthplace of the ego experience. When you focus your awareness on all the possibilities of the mind, you are not able to see your true self clearly and you now exist in an unawakened state of being or what you would call a mind-dominated state of being.

All the things that exist in the mind are simply witnessed by consciousness. All the thoughts of the mind that arise do so on their own 24/7. These thoughts arise as stored memories, stored concepts, stored knowledge, etc. They can be witnessed as individual knowledge or even group knowledge. Interconnectedness might play a factor if you are at a sporting event and your hometown team loses. Try to think about a riot at a sporting event. Even if all the participants are not violent people, the group-consciousness and their ego cling to that mob mentality as reality, and they might participate. It all stems from not knowing yourself enough to the point where you find yourself egoically doing things that you normally wouldn't do based on your reaction to your current surroundings. It all comes down to being stuck witnessing another mind-dominated state and reacting to it accordingly. To not get caught up in falling victim to the group-consciousness, you need to allow all things in the mind to arise without the immediate reaction that can spark something such as a riot.

One pointer that might help you understand that you are not the mind is to take a minute, close your eyes, and just tell the mind to "Stop." See if the mind follows your

instructions. Were you able to sit there quietly for a few minutes without any thoughts or mental dialog arising? If not, then hopefully can understand how out of control you are when dealing with the arising and subsiding of mental forms.

What happens when you meditate? The deeper you go, the more everything begins to shed away, right? This is why most people have a difficult time when they start meditating. They still believe themselves to be the mind and think that they are not good meditators because they are not able to focus enough to shut the mind off. They just haven't gone that deep or returned to the present moment enough to experience transcending the forms that they are always aware of. Most people give up before they get anywhere. They fail to realize that turning the mind off is an impossible task. It is only after many more meditation experiences that one can quietly witness the mind.

Touching the present moment by whatever means you use is the only place I know of where the mind isn't witnessed at all. Meditation is probably the easiest way to be fully present enough to gain an understanding of what true presence is because you're not being flooded with tons of form as you usually meditate in a quiet, peaceful place. In deep meditation, your awareness is focused on the knowingness that "I AM" instead of the uncertainty of "I THINK I AM." The "I AM" awareness or "BEINGNESS" of the present moment does not leave the door wide open for the mind to flood your awareness. Only when the changing mental forms of "I THINK I AM" are present, the door is left open for any number of mental concepts to arise to fill in the blank. I think I am a doctor; I think I am religious; I think I am spiritual; or I think therefore I am, etc. These mental concepts are considered reality only as long as you have a license to practice medicine, or as long as you belong to a religious organization, or as long as you keep up your spiritual practices, routines, and beliefs.

The ego illusions are simply changing mental forms that arise at any particular time to suit your current needs to define yourself as something or someone at that moment in time. Things are good when you have a license to practice medicine, so it feels good to proudly say I am a doctor. It is only after you lose your license to practice medicine that your ego diminishes enough to possibly return to the present moment where no definition of self is required. In the end, you will find that consciousness was always present during the arising and subsiding of outward forms and experiences. Whether you label your life experiences as good or bad, they are the same thing, taking different forms in the mind. This is why the ego is almost fully in control of every single person on earth because they fail to realize that the only differences between themselves and every single other person on earth are simply the changing mental/emotional/physical forms that are being witnessed.

The self-awareness that exists in the awakened state or the present moment is usually forced to take a back seat to all the possibilities of the mind. Your conscious awareness is now focused on giving certain mental concepts more meaning than others to make the present moment more desirable. Now the reality of good and bad, right and wrong, and all other concepts can come into play. All the things of the ego are offered up to the mind to play with in an attempt to make them a reality. Once the present moment is completely covered up by this mind-dominated state, separation from all others and your true self happens. Now the ego illusion is in full control, and you continue living out your life in this state of unawareness, chasing down better mental concepts than you have previously experienced.

Chapter 6

FEEDING THE MIND

FEEDING the mind is a common characteristic of the ego. It is that place in the mind/body where we all love to go to find ourselves or to break free from the troubles of the world. We try to get good at something to the point that it becomes effortless. We go deeper into the mind by feeding it things of form until we eventually witness freedom from the mind and enter a state of being that requires no thought or action.

For example, you could fully engross yourself mentally in a novel, a television series, a video game, or a movie. Have you noticed that when you are deeply entertained doing anything from reading a book, watching a movie, or playing a video game, you're not thinking about anything else? That state of non-awareness is feeding the mind. You are so intensely focused on whatever form you are witnessing that peace has the opportunity to arise, which is why people will get intensely caught up in the doing of it constantly and go deeper into the form it takes.

You can also fully engross yourself physically in things of form, such as weightlifting, running, swimming, dancing, etc. We have all read about a professional athlete who has gone so deeply into the form of running that running became effortless. Even though the mind and body might be fully consumed with the intensity of the outward action, and things are happening all around them, there is a huge space or gap between consciousness and the mind/body experience or the world of form. You kind of do something so much to where you feel free. The doing-ness of something becomes automatic, but the freedom experienced is probably what you are after. A lot of people consider this freedom talent, where it is completely effortless as it is happening.

These might sound like good things, but if you are seeking yourself in the world of form, you will only find a different aspect of your ego. You may experience the freedom that you already have at this very moment. However, you may assume that you need to go heavily into the world of form to find yourself or experience that peace or freedom, but you do not. There is no thinking or doing that is required to be fully present. This is another pointer to the world of opposites that we live in. We can either go heavily into the world of form to eventually find peace, or we can push the world of form away and find it just as easily.

Chapter 7

GETTING LOST IN THE WORLD OF FORM

THE WORLD of form is very seductive. It is the only thing you have ever known since birth or your first recollection of consciousness, that is. It is what keeps you from knowing your true self. The world of form is everything outward, such as thoughts, emotions, or the doing of something, etc. It can be your daily routines or your daily habits. Every single object that you can see with your eyes or touch with your body has a form. Every single thing you can taste with your mouth or everything you can hear with your ears has a form. Whatever it is that you smell right now has a form. There are no limits to the types of forms that can be witnessed, as every single thing contained in the mind/body experience has a form to it.

The world of form can be everything from getting up in the morning and having your first thoughts or feelings about how your day is going to go to making your first cup of coffee, taking a shower, and getting dressed. The point is when you are doing this day after day, there is no self-awareness present when navigating your way through this world of form. The mind views every single thing as something it has already labeled. You can stay lost in the world of form by surrounding yourself with forms that produce comforting thoughts, or you can get lost in searching for forms that are not yet known to the world. You can accept the world as already having been fully invented and you are just living in it, or you could lose yourself in continuing to invent more forms for the world.

Many of the forms we lose ourselves in daily are thought forms or concepts masquerading as professions. It could be waking up to save lives as a doctor, but since it has a form to it, there will always be an opposite. For all the lives you save, you will also witness the ending of others you can't save, even when you have done everything mentally right. This is a perfect example of thought forms producing suffering. When you have done everything perfectly in your mind to save someone and they still die, it produces suffering because you falsely believe that you are in total control of the situation based on all the outward knowledge you have collected through your education and applied to the particular situation that has always worked in the past.

The thought-form of being a doctor cannot exist unless you are willing to define yourself by the form you are losing yourself in. For example, while standing on the side of the road, a car accident happens right in front of you. You rush over and pull the victim out of the car, perform CPR, and save their life. Do you consider yourself to be a doctor? Of course, you don't, as you are not actively seeking yourself in the form of being a doctor; therefore, you will never have enough experiences that back up that belief. The structure of the ego is all about how you define yourself, and the doing of something that is needed to keep up that illusion. When the ego no longer maintains a form properly, such as a profession, then the illusion and ability to define yourself as that type of professional crumbles. A professional is someone who maintains a form to the best of their abilities. Can you imagine a doctor who dresses up like a clown before they go into the operating room to perform a procedure on you? You need to maintain the illusion of being a doctor to have patients to operate on. The interconnectedness of forms can easily be seen here as well. Without patients, a doctor can't be a doctor, can they?

Without an office, would you still want to see a doctor who is working out of the trunk of his car? Things of form are needed to keep up the illusion of being anything in life. Have you ever seen a professional skydiver that jumps out of a plane without a parachute? If a person jumped out of a plane without a parachute, the form would shift from a professional skydiver to a person who committed suicide. This is how extremely specific forms need to be to maintain the illusion that the form is an absolute reality. If you just change one aspect of the form, it automatically becomes something else.

Chapter 8

THE NATURE OF THE MIND AND FORM

Just to scratch the surface of the mind, try visualizing how many occupations there are in the world, try visualizing how many hobbies there are. Just the depths of those two forms alone are vast. If it helps, try to visualize the entire combined content of the internet stuffed into a container called the mind. That just scratches the surface of the nature of the mind. You probably don't realize it, but surfing the internet every single day for something new is the same thing taking on a different form. Each day might seem completely different as you are accessing different information based on what you witness arising in your mind at the time, but ultimately you are still sitting at your computer lost in thought, aren't you? This is how easy it is to get lost moving from one mental movement to the next as the form they take all seem different. You wouldn't consider riding a bicycle and jump roping to be the same thing, would you? Yet when you view it from the context of consciousness, aren't you witnessing two things arising in the mind and then reacting to the form it takes? Losing yourself in a form requires witnessing a thought arising and then some sort of reaction or doing based on that thought. Hopefully, that pointer makes it easier for you to understand when I say that even though they take on different forms. Ultimately, they are the same thing.

Realizing the depth of the mind-dominated state of consciousness can help you better understand how easy it is to remain completely separated from all others while you are completely consumed with living out your life in the world of form. It is getting lost in the world of form that causes this separation from all others. In the mind, how can you possibly look at another person who has taken a different form and consider them to be the same thing you are? How are you able to see clearly that they are doing the same thing you are and living life exactly as you have lived all this time when there are so many forms available to the mind that allow it to see others as something completely different? One person might go into the military, while another might choose to become a monk. They might seem like two entirely different life experiences where one might lead someone to war and the other to peace. Yet they both reacted to something that was witnessed arising in the mind and continued to follow the form until they were able to define themselves as each form. It is always the same thing for everyone. You follow a form long enough until you gain enough experience to be able to define yourself by that form. To see someone exercise daily and remain physically fit is no different from seeing someone overeat and gain weight. To see a separation between this form and that form keeps the cycle of human suffering going round and round. This separation is what causes the ego to react to maintain its position by believing it has made better choices than others. However, it fails to see that it has done the same thing in a different form. This is why only viewing the world through the eyes of the ego with limited beliefs, such as good or bad, no longer needs to be the only thing that makes us better than others. If we are not able to see others as we see ourselves, then we need to continue bringing awareness of this to one another from a place of compassion and not judgment. People do all kinds of different things, and nobody needs to be judged for their unawareness. The world of form is so vast that if we continue to label every single thing contained within it, it will only drive us further apart as conscious beings witnessing a human experience.

If a person says something to you that causes an instantaneous defensive reaction, that is your ego. The need to react is what needs awareness brought to it, not the form of the reaction which makes them seem completely different.

Whoever thought that an argument could be used as a tool for truly understanding yourself? If you say something nice instead of negatively reacting, yet inside you are thinking all the things you want to say, that is a different form of ego as well.

Most people egoically put on a happy face while they are miserable inside. Most people don't even listen to what is being said to them half the time. They may be witnessing negative thoughts the moment you say something, or they are busy witnessing their reaction formulating in the mind. If they have labeled you negatively, they will automatically negatively respond to you. Your ego will attempt to pick apart that form to maintain your own and vice versa. Their viewpoint is not valid as it is coming from a place of complete unawareness, just as your negative viewpoint of them is not valid. You will know how unaware you are when you stop in the middle of putting them down and realize you weren't actually thinking about the true depth of the suffering you might cause them. You were simply just doing it automatically, without any self-awareness involved. The mental attachment to form needs to jump from one thing to the next without any gaps in between, which is why it is so easy to fight with someone. If you were both willing to continue the storyline, you might go back and forth for hours if nobody stops you. Arguing is a form all on its own. We all know how easy it is to lose ourselves in an argument to the point where we end up saying something we would never say. That experience is just another aspect of getting lost in the world of form. The true depth of the world of form covers every single experience you can have in this life from birth until death.

Any form has a set pattern of events that need to happen perfectly for the illusion of that form to sustain itself. For example, let's say you went grocery shopping. First, you enter the store, select your groceries, and then pay for them at the checkout stand. Those specific events that happen in that order make up the form of grocery shopping. If one event in the entire sequence doesn't happen, then the form changes and you could easily go from grocery shopping to stealing if you don't pay for the food.

The biggest problem that arises when the ego is fully in control is that it requires no thought or effort on your part, and it also doesn't need to include anybody else in your routines. It happens spontaneously based on past conditioning and past routines. It requires no true self-awareness to be present and no love or compassion toward others or even yourself. It is what you would call mechanical in nature.

To help you get away from being stuck on autopilot, you need to know that consciousness is always present first. If you are living presently, then you can witness going from form to form. If you are not, then you can easily find yourself lost in the world of form. If we believe ourselves to be this mind and this body and the various forms they both take, we completely miss the awareness of actually being conscious in the present moment. So, remember that consciousness always exists first, and then the world of form arises for us to witness second. It is important not to discount the aliveness that we already are without needing anything in the world of form to prove it. We get stuck in a never-ending cycle of the ego being completely in control of jumping from one form to the next every day of our lives if we lose our presence.

When this happens, we lose our ability to choose what we want to experience while navigating the world of form, and unfortunately, the world of form chooses for us based on our current surroundings/situations and past mental conditioning. We become a slave to our egos when no self-awareness is present. The ego always needs to maintain its dominance in the present moment. If you are challenged in any way, you automatically go into a defensive mindset. The ego hardly wants to share its mental space with anybody else's views; that is why two conflicting viewpoints hardly ever share the same time and space without being a problem. If one person begins arguing, then the other either chooses to react out of ego or chooses a non-reaction out of self-awareness. The more we get lost in the world of form, the longer we will continue to cause suffering for ourselves and others around us. All the time that is spent in the world of form is what keeps us from truly knowing our deepest non-reactive selves.

Ask yourself why you only know good or bad. Even a terrorist considers themselves to be doing good works for whatever their purpose is.

Ask yourself why there is a need to pick a side. Why have you not stood in the middle and looked to the left, then looked to the right and realized that both directions require some sort of doing to get to your destination? Why haven't you realized that you only need one experience in the eyes of another to be labeled good in this world as you also only need one experience to be labeled bad? The middle path is an awareness of both extremes of the mind that doesn't require any doing to attain; it is always here waiting for you. You will see that non-reaction produces good things easier than reactions based on good thoughts.

We need to learn how to share the mental space that the ego seeks to dominate. If we make allowances for all things contained in the mind to exist without automatically positioning a self on one side of the line or the other, we will experience a lot more peace in this world. If only the form of sharing or co-existing as equals had arisen back at the beginning of recorded history and not the need to continually dominate in one form or another based on good or bad, right or wrong, the world would be different today with such examples of compassion for all of humanity.

Chapter 9

THE EGO IS A TACO

I'll try to give you some more pointers that might be easier to understand by using the metaphor of the ego being a taco. As we all know, there are endless ways of creating an amazing taco. You have tons of choices about what ingredients you wish to put on your taco. First, you start by browning some hamburger. At this point, you can add any kind of seasoning you desire, or you can choose to add none. Then you select either a hard shell or a soft shell. You can add cheese and sour cream or ketchup or lettuce.

The list can go on and on, but in the end, the taco of your choosing will always consist of the total of all ingredients that you desire based on your past conditioning. You usually make the taco like you always have, or you can also choose to add something new to the mix to make a different type of taco. It all comes down to how you feel during the moment you are making it, but in the end, a taco is still a taco, no matter how you make it.

The same is true for the ego experience. You can go through your entire life adding different outward ingredients that create your inward concept of who you think you are. Keep in mind that the structure of the ego consists of all the concepts that exist in the mind. The ego is constantly seeking change and constantly seeking the next best thing, so you keep adding different ingredients to produce a better life for yourself.

Ultimately, there is no difference in the ingredients you choose as it will all come down to your individual mental beliefs based on your concept of what is better or worse for you. Once you have taken the total of these mental opinions and lumped them together to form your ego, you will now have completed your taco.

Its taste and desirability will dictate how long you choose to experience your life by either clinging to the same ingredients or choosing to create a different taco altogether. In the end, the ego will always be the same thing; it will just take different forms, which will always be the reason why one way to live will be more desirable than another. The problem is mankind will never be united until we are all aware that we are all living the same taco experience with slightly different ingredients. An example of the different tacos.

Chapter 10

THE EGOIC RIVALRY

The egoic conditioning that we all experience plays itself out selfishly in the form of habits or routines, including mental, physical, and even emotional. Each ego will culminate in a different form, but no matter what form it takes, the ego will seek separation from all others to some extent so that it can remain unique. The mind-dominated ego requires some sort of difference between yourself and the next person, and this difference will only exist in the world of form, such as clothes or hobbies, careers, mental beliefs, addictions, desires, etc. There is no limit to the form it could take, but a separation of some sort will always be present in a mind-dominated state of consciousness.

For example, the mind might lead you to believe that no two fishermen could be exactly alike or have the same skill level at catching fish because the competitive ego requires that somebody has to eventually be better than the other. The ego can only maintain this structural belief based on the proof that a storyline provides. Without a storyline, how is it possible to know who has outperformed the other? Since the mind loves to live in the past, it believes that it has the track record to prove it based on previous fishing trips, so the competitive ego clings heavily to past fishing trips to derive its solidity. The only reason this solidity seems like absolute reality is because of the mental differences that arise after comparing the forms that each person's fishing experience has taken. The more you start to compare all things such as boats and crews and numbers caught, the less you can see the consciousness that you both share, so it begins to seem impossible to be the same thing taking on a different form. The full-on witnessing of the mind-dominated state of consciousness is the cause of the separation and all the differentiated beliefs. I mean, right off the bat, if you just have one thing different, like a boat, then how could you possibly be the same? In the mind, one boat has to be bigger or better than the other. One boat will be faster, or it might hold more fish. As each thought continues to rise, so does the separation from one another as being the same, taking on a different form. As more thoughts of me and mine are added to the concept of being a better fisherman, the unconditional love and compassion for the other fisherman are covered up with the awareness that I can't help him catch more fish when we are competing because I can't lose. It is almost as if during the competition they are practically enemies, even if they don't wish physical harm to each other.

In this full awareness of the ego experience, each person believes that no matter how many fish are caught, someone has to be better than the other. The mental concept gives rise to keeping score. So even though both of them might be catching fish, neither would consider the other person at the same skill level; therefore competition, to a certain extent, will always be present.

What you ultimately have is two competing mental egoic thought forms. You have two fishermen in mind-dominated states of consciousness that have two completely different egos firmly in place, and each ego desires to win in some way over the next competing ego. This holds in all forms of life, not just with fishing. Think of race car drivers or professional gamblers. We all know the list could be endless as everything in the ego experience is a competition to some degree.

Can you begin to see how the egoic separation occurs because of the mental belief that we are all individuals and no two people on earth are created the same, not even identical twins? Instead of having two fishermen considering themselves to be brothers and united through consciousness, two egoic rival fishermen are competing for the same fish in the same waters. Eventually, one of them will have to do better or be better than the other, no matter how friendly they are toward each other. They could even be brothers doing this to one another. This mentality is what opens the door to suffering because you are living in the mind, and you are living in the future hoping to catch more. If for some reason you don't end up catching more, some form of suffering arises to the point that your ego redefines itself to not lose any mental ground. We all know that when you lose you don't want to step backward in life, which is why you usually end up blaming something or someone for the loss. After you lose, you might begin to think, "Well I didn't catch more than him, but I caught enough so I'm happy." That simple example points to all the shifting mind movements from moment to moment. Things are constantly arising and changing the outcome of how your mind forms its ego-self, which is always in a constant state of reaction to outward stimuli. Ultimately both fishermen lost in this example; they were stuck living in the ego experience the entire fishing trip. When you live your life in the mind like this you open yourself up to opposites. No matter if both wanted to feel like winners, one would feel victorious and the other would feel sad and discouraged for having lost the opportunity to prove himself to be the better fisherman. Unfortunately, both failed to realize that they could have experienced extreme peace and love the entire time regardless of the outcome. Competition isn't necessarily a bad thing, but when you define yourself by the outcome, then it simply allows suffering to continue to arise in your life.

The only way the world of opposites would not hold is if one of the two fishermen was fully self-aware and had no desire to be separate or to seek separation through mental means and outward action or circumstances. The joy and peace of being fully present while fishing is rewarding enough and needs no definition or distinction between others. The self-aware or enlightened fisherman is not seeking to find himself in the form of fishing itself, he is already found existing before any form ever has the opportunity to arise at this moment. The enlightened fisherman has come full circle and is once again just witnessing the act of fishing as it's happening without clinging to the thought that he has found himself in it and proudly proclaims I am a "better fisher-man," even if he does it for a living and makes a lot of money at it. At the end of the day, for an enlightened fisherman, fishing is just fishing; anything else added on top of that is more ego accumulating and causing separation from other fishermen and the present moment.

Chapter 11

EGO AND ENEMIES

In the ego experience, there is a natural need to create enemies. When you are in a mind-dominated state of consciousness, you naturally need everything to be done perfectly, otherwise an enemy is created.

Enemies can take so many forms that the concept of time can even become an enemy. How many people do you know that are constantly running late and constantly missing appointments or even getting fired at work because they can't seem to remain present enough to keep their focus on what time it is? The ego works hard to remain firmly rooted in being on the side of good, no matter what the enemy turns out to be. Your ego believes that they are good or correct, and it will naturally react to someone or something that is not as good or right. For the person who gets fired for being late all the time, do they believe they had anything to do with it? Or do they have a ton of excuses for why they could never be on time? Their ego will never admit that they are wrong because they think the circumstances are out of their control. They know that they are not exactly right for being late, but they still don't think they are wrong. Without someone or something being bad or wrong, how could you possibly remain good or right? The mind-dominated state usually only finds peace after a victory of some form, even if it's a tiny victory, like convincing your boss that your kids were to blame for you being late for work. It is only this ego-self that will ever experience having an enemy of any sort because it is the only part of your awareness that constantly denies the present moment. The deepest part of you that witnesses the ego is the only part that will never truly know an enemy, as it never denies the present moment. The concept of a true enemy only exists in the mind, anyway. A true enemy is the opposite of a mental belief that you hold to be good or absolutely right. It is a denial of the present moment in whatever form it takes that leads you to believe that it is somehow wrong, which makes your ego instinctively fight for survival by remaining right or better.

Luckily, the thought of an enemy is mind-created, which is why eventually it too will subside, and you no longer cling to the illusion. If you are enemies with someone, then you will see that the moment that neither of you is willing to keep up the illusion that you are both enemies. If one of you starts acting compassionately towards the other person, the illusion will crumble. The illusion is only able to last as long as you both continue playing out the storyline of enemies.

You can only have an enemy for as long as you mentally cling to the negative thoughts or concepts. The other person or thing never truly needs to change. It is your willingness to let go of the mental attachment to such beliefs that change. If a person or a thing has become an enemy, it is only because of your denial of the present moment that has created such beliefs in your mind and the storyline that you are willing to maintain. The more aggressively you push it away in your mind, the stronger the denial gets. When you deny the present moment, no matter what form it takes, you naturally believe that you have somehow been wronged, or you feel forced to deal with something or someone that you don't want to. The ego experience is all about agreement with others. The moment you stop agreeing with someone, you start to witness a mental enemy. You might begin to believe that the enemy is the opposite of what you are or want to be. You no longer experience unconditional love and acceptance the moment you begin judging someone or something. When you view another person from the standpoint of your ego-self, you naturally compare their actions and their behaviors to your own; that is how an enemy is born. It doesn't have to be an accumulation of events that leads up to feeling discomfort and the desire to completely avoid someone or something. It can happen instantly as well, but you will see that no matter how it comes about you begin to judge something from the eyes of the ego. You automatically begin labeling and comparing what you consider to be an enemy to the self that you have created in your mind. You pit your ego against their ego and use their words and actions as ammunition to maintain the separation you experience in your mind. You will see that it only exists in your mind in that particular form when you ask someone else what they think of the other person. The form the other person has taken in their mind might be completely different.

If the other person makes a mistake and you are so disgusted with them over it, you have pitted your ego-self against someone who has already done the unthinkable, which stems from their unawareness. If given the choice to do it again, do you think they would choose to do it all over? They were probably lost in the motion of the ego experience and that unawareness can lead to tremendous suffering. If you just saw them through unconditionally loving and accepting eyes, then you would realize that no matter what they have done or will do, you are only truly battling your egoic attachment to the mind. If you were to allow self-awareness to return to the present moment and to practice non-reaction, then you would see that just as quickly as they made a mistake. You can also quickly resist the immediate urge to react. It is through this non-reaction that you witness the arising and subsiding of the ego-self. Just as quickly as you do not react, you will witness the mind subsiding. New space will enter the situation that will allow you to continue to experience unconditional love and compassion for all. Hopefully, in that non-reaction, you will see that the entire struggles of the mind/body experience only exist in the mind. The true road to self-awareness is through non-reaction, which is the same as unconditional love and compassion. True unconditional love and compassion are simply awareness that someone might have done something they shouldn't have, but no amount of denying their form will ever change what they did. Instead, you simply acknowledge what was done with the gentle non-reactive self that is at your core and you make space in your immediate awareness for it to exist without the need to change it. You will see that true unconditional love and compassion allows the person who offers it to remain in a state of peaceful presence and the receiver of it is still typically stuck in the past over what they did so it doesn't have to mean anything in the mind such as you accept what they did as right.

Peace is found within you as the other person might not even offer the mental peace that you are attempting to give them.

There is nothing that is given other than non-reaction which is in itself nothingness in a sense. They might feel unbalanced from their actions, but why do you instantly require your own unbalance to prove that what they did was wrong?

Mental enemies could be a person, place, or thing that was witnessed at the time your egoic standards might have considered the problem. However, you have to look deeper to see the truth that the enemy was neither right nor wrong. You just simply reacted again instantly without any self-awareness present. For most people, a spontaneous outburst in a negative manner will cause your ego to defend its position to justify the reaction. You can either choose to be the vessel of anger and unforgiveness toward another person and mentally consider them an enemy, or you can look beyond the egoic differences and forms to see them for the very same thing that you are which allows unconditional love and compassion to arise in the present moment. The whole point of taking the time to practice non-reaction and acceptance is to continue to end the suffering that you experience in your life. We all know how sickening it feels to get around someone you consider an enemy. Imagine if you were able to gain true awareness of the nature of your mind to stop living in it. Imagine if you were so completely one with yourself that the arising and subsiding of the mind were no longer able to cause you any suffering in any area of your life. That is the place that humanity is gravitating toward.

Space is opening up in our conscious awareness that will allow this process to keep unfolding in the mind/body experience. It is already happening in your life; you probably just don't have the proper context to put it in yet. Unconditional love for yourself and all others is again

NON-REACTION. The next time someone makes a statement that triggers your ego to defend itself, take a breath and realize their opinion is just as valid to them as your opinion is to you. Their opinion is not absolute reality, which is why your ego needs no true defense. Their opinion stems from their ego, and that is all based on the culmination of their experiences. This is why words truly only have the power over you that you give them. The more you react, the more power you give other people's words and conceptualized ideas about you.

The more unbalanced you become, the more you are allowing their ego to think what they have said is proof that they were right.

Just let things be and exist just as they are without the egoic need to change them. You will see that in the end, it is not the world of form that changes, meaning other people's negative thoughts or all the outward suffering that you see in the world will end, but it is your non-reaction to the world of form that ultimately ends the suffering for you. When this personal suffering has ended, then all enemies have been defeated and other people can do and say whatever they want, and it won't control you. They will no longer be the puppet master pulling on the strings of your ego. You are now free to spread unconditional love and peace because you truly know what they mean. It is only when you become aware of your mental suffering that you can then help point it out to others to help them end their suffering as well. You don't end suffering by paying someone's bills that they can't afford as that only produces mental peace. You are instead teaching them that peace is always present, no matter what is arising in their life. We have all heard the proverb, *"Give someone a fish and you feed him for a day; teach someone to fish and you feed him for a lifetime."* The same thing in a different form could be, "Pay someone's bills and give him peace for a day; Teach someone unconditional love and acceptance of the present moment and give him peace for a lifetime."

Peace is a state of being that just is. Peace is your normal state before the ego-self ever enters your conscious awareness and starts to add things of form that take you further away from that natural state of being. Peace of mind is a mental state that arises after opposing forces that are no longer experiencing friction subside. Comparing true peace and mental peace is like comparing apples and oranges; it just doesn't work. Mental peace and mental conflict are still the same thing taking on different forms, so it is like comparing apples to apples only one apple is green when the other is red, so they seem different. When peace of mind is experienced, you only witness your release of whatever was bothering you. When an enemy says they are sorry and peace of mind is experienced, you can consider that a release of some form of denial. You are simply returning to the present moment by releasing the clinging to the mental enemy that was bothering you. Hopefully, you can see the difference as true peace was something you had before, during, and after the conflict only you didn't know it was still there because it was covered up by all the mental form that was clung to during the period of mental unrest. Whereas, peace of mind is something that is found on the other side of the conflict as it depends on the releasement of the conflicting mental forms that were causing you problems. When one mind movement subsides, another form arises to take its place in your immediate awareness. The egoic labels that are placed on each movement whether it is good or bad are not important as you need to become aware of what mental form is.

To label someone an enemy is to give the conceptualized person that is created in your mind a negative thought form. You need to move beyond what you see with your eyes and what you have known to be true about them, as it is all useless in the present moment. How are you to ever allow them to show you a different side of themselves if you are always coming at them with anger or hatred based on past events? Isn't it expected that they would have an attitude if you treated them poorly or didn't even acknowledge their presence? How would their behavior change if you were to smile and say hi to them no matter what has happened in the past? We all can change at the drop of a hat. That instant change is made possible by releasing the ego and returning to the present moment. Who you were yesterday is not who you are today. You could have always been an extremely angry person with serious anger management issues, but the moment you bring awareness to how your ego uses the form of anger as a tool for survival is the moment you can release the egoic attachment to it and slowly return to the present moment where anger only exists as a mental concept of the ego.

How you acted in high school is not how you act today.

To say someone is a bad person because of something they did in the past is only another denial of the present moment on your part. I'm not saying that if someone has done something terrible to you that you need to prove that you are living presently by allowing them back into your life with open arms as that is another form of ego and can continue to cause you more harm. What I am saying is, to find peace with the thought that they too are allowed to exist wherever they are in the world no matter what form they take. We have all heard of the concept of karma and people pretty much live their karma in a way. You don't need to be angry at someone or punish them as their own beliefs typically do that in all areas of their life to a far greater extent than what you could ever do. The mind they have created based on their past actions could be far worse than what you have created about them in your mind. They could experience their own suffering based on their negative thoughts. So why do you feel the need to join them by reacting to your negative thoughts? You need to make room in your mind for them to exist, which is the only way to find peace for yourself. It is only when you deny their right to exist as they are that you could find yourself doing something terrible like causing them unneeded suffering or even killing them. The only true separation between us and others is made possible by looking at them as a mind-dominated conceptualized form.

The separation between the present moment and being lost in the mind-dominated state of consciousness is pretty easy to see when you are angry and unbalanced. It is not easily seen when the form is good-natured, like having a best friend. Best friends can cause you just as much suffering as enemies, even if it takes on a form that you want more than anything. You will never see the problem in this until someone is holding a gun to your head and asking you to choose between allowing your best friend to live or a perfect stranger. Now think of who you would choose and why. Now ask yourself. What if you knew the stranger, and they were your mortal enemy? How much of an easier choice would it be to pick your best friend? This is how the ego operates. It always needs to make a choice based on good or bad, right or wrong. Luckily, this is not a literal example, and hopefully, nobody would ever have to make any choices of that nature, but it points to the mental form that people take in our minds. If we do not understand how the ego operates, then how are we to truly understand how to regain awareness of the present moment? The only thing that allows you to choose your best friend over a stranger is the mental form you have created. The reason that going to the extreme side of what makes you happy is not any better than going to the extreme side of what makes you sad is they both can cause you tremendous suffering. Even when you have an extremely deep mental attachment to the form of something good, the moment you take that form completely away is the moment deep suffering can also arise. Do you see how the ego is existing in a world of opposites? Something you consider so amazingly good can cause you just as much suffering as something that you consider to be so amazingly bad.

Chapter 12

TALENT vs. ADDICTION

Since the mind/body experience is open to the world of opposites, you have to be very careful how you go about viewing mental concepts and perceptions of yourself and all others in your mind. I heard a quote once that said something to the effect of, "The difference between heaven and hell is only an eighth of an inch apart." The same is true for any good or bad concept that is held in the mind.

Once again, the only difference between this concept and that concept is the context in which it is held. The difference between talent and addiction depends on the context in which it is held as well. In this case, the context of good vs. bad, right vs. wrong, healthy vs. unhealthy, etc. For instance, if a person were so heavily focused on the form of golf, let's say, then most people would call this talent. A person can be so heavily focused on one thing that they can become a professional at doing it. Keep in mind that it is only considered a profession if the form it takes is deemed socially good, right, healthy, etc.

The opposite of what is considered talent, depending on the good or bad context that you hold this in, could also be called addiction. When a person is focused heavily on a form that the group consciousness of a particular society considers to be negative, the person is no longer considered talented; they are now considered addicted.

Ultimately, they are just addicted to a form that is not socially accepted. As we all know, there may be professional addicts out there, but because the ego is firmly in place with almost all people, that need for separation from one another is now given another opportunity to arise. The feeling that I am better than that person arises, and the ego is now once again secure in whoever is witnessing the addict seeking themselves in what the mind calls all the wrong places. Can you imagine there being something like the National Drug Abuse League where professional drug abusers challenge each other to see who can do more drugs than the other person? How can the ego survive in a world where negative things like drug addictions are celebrated like they celebrate a golf addict? How would you feel if a major drug addict was considered equal in the eyes of the world to who you are? How would you feel if you were considered equal to the best golfer in the world? Hopefully, you can see that the ego automatically doesn't feel as bad if it is compared to something it considers to be good because it doesn't require a defense. It does not need to fight for survival if it is still good in the eyes of others, but the moment you are compared with something bad, then watch out as the ego, if challenged enough, will fight to the death to maintain its mental position.

We all know that addictions can take unlimited forms from sex addiction to drug and alcohol addiction to whatever form that is held in a negative context. Even mental addictions and disorders all have a form to them. A person who is considered mentally insane ultimately could be considered an addict to the mind by having witnessed an uncontrollable desire to remain lost in it or to say they have gone a lot deeper into the witnessing than most and continue to react to the depth of that witnessing. Being labeled mentally insane is only possible by having an opposite awareness or a person judging them based on their mental balance. Once again, can you imagine having the National League of the Mentally Insane where people compete to see who is considered more insane than the other? The ego loves competition no matter what form it takes so this too would even gain popularity and have a following.

The problem with allowing this egoic separation to occur is that people viewed as talented are accepted by society and the people labeled with addictions are not. I'm not saying that it is okay to have addictions, as all addictions in any form keep you away from the present moment. I'm not saying that talent is not okay to have either, as many beautiful things arise in the present moment from talented people. I'm saying that compassion needs to arise for the talented person just as much as the addicted person by realizing that both are seeking themselves in the same way through different forms. When you go to one extreme in any form, there is always an opportunity to experience the exact opposite. For a talented person, the opposite might be a fall from grace. For an addict, the opposite might be returning to the soberness of the present moment. We have all seen movies where a super-talented person has ended up having a mental breakdown because they couldn't deal with their enormous success, and they ended up locking themselves in a house for the rest of their life never wanting to leave. On the flip side, we have all seen a movie where a person with a major negative addiction was able to return to the present moment and kick their addiction and in the process began teaching others how to avoid the same addictions. No matter what scenario plays out for the person that society considers talented or addicted, the point is that both extremes leave the door wide open to suffering if neither learns how to return to the present moment. Unfortunately, we all know that group consciousness has always drawn a mental line in the sand between good and bad, and people are treated accordingly.

This line doesn't leave room for compassion to arise as the viewpoint of good or right is always pitted against the viewpoint of bad or wrong.

Compassion is the middle path of unity amongst all beings no matter what form they take. I know most people would think that hardcore drug addicts made their choice, but hopefully, after reading this book, you might begin to understand that the cut-and-dry viewpoint of the ego is only one awareness of the mind-dominated state of consciousness. Luckily, the more each of us returns to the present moment, the more dimensions of consciousness begin to expose themselves to our immediate awareness. If someone wasn't living presently, then did they choose to completely lose themselves in a major addiction that could end their life, or was it their ego-self that always craves more or better experiences all the while denying what it currently has? Unfortunately, in most cases, there is the egoic sense that I'm on the good side of the line so I'm doing okay, but since you are on the bad side of the line, you are on your own and I don't want to be associated with you. Each of us has a responsibility to continue creating space in our consciousness for all things to exist to reach that state of non-reaction. If you can stop judging based on a good or bad form, then you can see talent vs. addiction as the same thing taking on a different form. When that happens, you will no longer feel the egoic pull to celebrate talent so heavily or deny addiction so heavily as you will be able to easily see the middle path of compassion for how heavily each group is focused on a particular form. Not everybody who praises a talented person when times are good will love them the same when times turn bad. This is the separation that the ego causes. Regardless of the form the ego takes, both a drug addict and an athlete still equally deserve love and compassion. The drug addict is no longer able to control their egoic desires to escape reality any more than an athlete feels a deep desire to play their sport. The same thing is happening to both of them, but it only looks different on the outside.

Chapter 13

DENIAL LEADS TO SUFFERING

THE BIGGEST NEMESIS to the ego is another ego that clings to opposing mental concepts. On one hand, you have a single person or a group of people who cling heavily to a certain set of concepts and have labeled that the proper way to live life or experience the present moment. On the other hand, you have another person or group who has opposing concepts that cling to a different way to live life or experience the present moment that they consider better.

Ultimately, what you have is two opposing mind-dominated states of consciousness that are doing the same thing. Instead, they are using different forms to define themselves. It is kind of like saying there are two opposing forms using different languages to tell the same story, only neither side realizes this because they are both so heavily focused on the different forms or languages that they are using themselves. Self-awareness is not present enough to see the similarities between enemies, because the ego thrives on differences. It all comes down to past mental conditioning for both opposing parties. Their surroundings or environment in which they were raised will dictate which concepts, rituals, and ceremonies were taught to them from the previous generations and defined as the proper way to live life.

Basically, the ego experience is the total of all past mind/body experiences lumped together and called "me," "life," or "my life." When you have an opposing force to this concept of life or the ideas and beliefs that you have come to hold dear to your heart, then naturally conflict and suffering arise. Instead of seeing an egoic enemy as the same thing that you are only taking on a different form, the ego instead sees an individual or a group of individuals separate from yourself. They can threaten the peace and comfort that you have found in the mind by clinging to certain concepts that you have mentally ruled better than others based on the past.

You can see these egoic rivalries in friendships and relationships on a personal level, or in larger groups or organizations and governments on more of a group consciousness level. I call these conflicting points of view "rivalries" because ultimately egos are competing to dominate the present moment.

Nobody who has made an enemy of the present moment will ever really win anything by doing so. In the mind, a belief might arise that you got the better of someone or you won a confrontation, but that is never the case. That is simply another arising thought form of a mind-dominated state of witnessed consciousness. When these egoic conflicts arise, they can produce suffering on various levels, depending on how many other egos agree with the original concept that sparked a mental enemy. Egoic concepts can be small and individual points. A person can be labeled shy for their lack of willingness to share their concepts with others, or they can be huge and encompass an entire civilization at which point one country could go to war with another country over different viewpoints.

This is the problem with lacking the awareness to be present enough to ultimately see an enemy as a denial of the present moment and the forms that are arising as the same thing. The ego is so heavily focused on the illusion of itself that not one single thought is given to the amount of suffering that is produced by such a denial of the present moment in any form it takes. Not only do other people end up suffering from your actions and reactions, but you suffer as well when self-awareness slowly returns, and you realize how out of control you actually were when you said or did things to hurt others.

Chapter 14

REACTION VS. NON-REACTION

IN THE HISTORY OF MANKIND, the unfortunate choice to do nothing has hardly been an option. The mind-dominated state of consciousness needs to have its opposing forces available at all times. In the mind, you believe if you do not act first out of fear you might lose, or if you don't act in retaliation, then you are being taken advantage of. When true self-awareness is present, you have the choice to act out the illusions of the ego or you can simply choose to remain present where no action or reaction is required. It is only the false sense of self that needs to defend the mental concept of "YOU" that is created throughout your lifetime. As you surround yourself with more people, the focus of an individual "You" shifts to the group consciousness of "Us," and this increases the potential for suffering tremendously.

Some people are being taught the mental concept of "an eye for an eye," or that the punishment needs to be equivalent to, if not greater than, the injury. This mental belief is based on the concept that the ego needs protection, because if we do not protect this mental concept of the self or the group, then fear and unknowingness would arise, and the illusion of the conceptualized form would begin to crumble. We would feel lost if we had nothing to gain or lose or nothing to do or fight for. If in the mind-dominated state of consciousness, we had no purpose, then what is the point of living? Where would the ego find its importance? Why would there be a need for an ego if there were no opposing mental forces in play at all times?

The ego's focus is to fight for survival. That is why the ego needs to have enemies. If none are readily available, then enemies can easily be created in the mind. What is the enemy of having fun? Work, of course. Do you see how easy it is to create suffering in one's life simply by needing to have enemies? Work is usually what allows you the ability to afford to have certain types of fun, but when you are busy working, it sure seems like the biggest enemy to the present moment, doesn't it? All of these mental enemies usually stem from denying the present moment, no matter what form it takes. Once you know this, then you can begin to see it in every action and reaction of all the surrounding people who are denying the present moment, because they are making their way through the day, creating suffering wherever they go.

For example, in reality shows where a guy propositions a girl at a bar, her ego, in turn, throws her drink in the guy's face for even suggesting such a thing. She has denied the present moment and made an enemy out of it. First, the mental form of the ego arises and is witnessed, then an instinctual reaction is experienced as the drink is thrown in his face based on past decisions that have been made. Leading to the belief that she is a certain type of woman who would never even consider such a thing. When the ego is fully in control like this, no thought is given in this type of situation; there is only an action that causes an egoic reaction, and that reaction can lead to more suffering and violence.

The opposite example would be for the man to proposition a self-aware woman. The self-aware woman might witness the egoic thoughts arising but not react to them. She could then choose to decline his invitation very kindly, and in doing so, no suffering or violence would arise. Both examples point to the mental state of either clinging to a very heavy false sense of self or knowing that a very diminished sense of self needs no defense. Ultimately, the first example is simply an example of a woman defending a mental concept of who she thinks she is. The reality could be different, but in that moment a heavy egoic sense of self was witnessed arising and was reacted upon with zero awareness of the present moment.

Take these two examples and change the context back to one nation throwing a drink in another nation's face, and now hopefully you can see that the reaction is the same thing, only it can take on a much more devastating form. Reaction vs. non-reaction ultimately will come down to who is more aware of the self and the present moment and who is completely lost in the illusions of the ego and stuck in the mind, defending concepts.

Chapter 15

MENTAL CREATION

MENTAL CREATION IS another form that the ego loves to keep you lost in. Let's say you invented the first computer, or the first car, or airplane. The concept arises that without the egoic "you" in this world, whatever you created would never have come into existence or taken form.

Now importance is given to your ego, and you have now become an "important" person. The mental creation has now given rise to the thought that you are better than the next person somehow because you are now an important part of human history. The ego can feel like it's finally made it, only when outward circumstances support the thought, and also when other people in the world agree.

The ego is now beginning to build stronger illusions, which, in turn, produce a bigger separation from all other people in the world. For example, you could have previously considered yourself lower to middle class, but after the invention took off, you could now consider yourself upper class.

Before you experienced the process of creating something new, you were not so separated from others. After possible fame and fortune accompanied this new creation, a bigger and bigger separation from others occurs in all kinds of different ways.

When once you could have gone to the grocery store to buy food, now you no longer can, possibly because of fame, or you no longer need to because you have hired a personal chef. At one point in time, you were able to give a person a ride home who was walking down the side of the road in the rain, but you no longer can because of security reasons. Fear always accompanies an inflated ego, because now you believe you have more to lose than a homeless person begging for money at a stoplight.

These mind-created attachments to the world of form run deeply in this state of consciousness.

Your awareness of others or connection with others is now shrinking more and more into just the thought of you alone. You now go through a process of creating a better life for yourself alone, not giving any thought to others who are suffering in the world. Since everything has an opposite, you could also experience giving so much thought to others in the world that you, in turn, experience suffering and are all alone. Usually, it is only after you have gone so deeply into the ego experience, enough to feel completely secure for life, does your awareness of others slowly returns. Now begins a process of giving back after you have received or taken so much from the world of form.

The separation that occurs when the ego is inflated so heavily between you and others really only exists in the mind. The mind itself loves to create new thought forms twenty-four hours a day. The ego believes that because outward circumstances are changing in your life; it is somehow making you into the person you want to be. Success is the fuel that the ego requires to feel secure.

Egoic desires are witnessed in the mind, and when the desires are not fulfilled, suffering occurs. The ego always desires to win, always desires to succeed, grow, progress, etc. When outward circumstances are in alignment with this mind-dominated state, we feel that everything is perfect, fantastic, or amazing. Yet when things are not going our way outwardly, our egos begin to suffer, and we don't feel so secure in the mind anymore, and self-defeating thoughts can slowly begin to creep into our awareness.

The ego only tends to give out generosity when it feels completely secure, otherwise clinging or grasping at things of form occurs. Only when that mental security is witnessed once again, that we begin the process of releasing the attachment to the ego to allow room to help others. This is why mental creation comes in many forms, from creating something outwardly such as a computer, or inwardly such as the thought that you are so incredibly important that you need to hire ten security guards to protect you at all times. At the end of the day, simply create the kind of reality that you want to experience. Don't let your ego take control and create a reality where you eventually look back and realize you have left nothing but pain and suffering in the pursuit of your egoic desires.

Chapter 16

INNOVATION AND THE EGO

In the mind-dominated state of consciousness, the ego will always need or desire more. The ego needs to go deeper into the mind in search of itself. The thought of innovation is one place the ego can go deeper that has no limits because the very concept of innovation has no end. It is one of those concepts like science or medicine that can be taken deeper and deeper with seemingly no possible end to it. In the ego experience, something new can always be created or discovered.

The ego is constantly in search of the next best thing. There has to be a progression to the mind-dominated state of consciousness or a continuation from one thing to the next, to the next, to the next, all the way until physical death. The egoic desire to need more or have more or search for more is always one of the most important pursuits of the ego.

It's happening all around you daily and most people fail to see it, simply because they are so dominated by this state of consciousness. People usually consider this state normal in everyday life. They will give it zero attention, and it has the potential to dominate your entire life, from birth until death.

When the desire arises to innovate something or to bring about something completely new, the ego will usually be in control. You will get lost in the doing, or the thinking, or the progression that is unfolding in the mind, and mistakenly believe that the egoic "you" is the one that is making all the innovation possible. Huge thoughts of grandeur are usually present.

Thoughts like "I AM" making history, "I AM" changing the world, etc. The ego experience always has a sense of importance attached to it, no matter what you are doing.

The failure to see the consciousness that exists before anything in the mind even has a chance to arise is how the ego will dominate the experience and zero self-awareness will be present during the unfolding of the mind in the present moment. Your true self-awareness is lost in the progression of the thoughts or the doing-ness as it is happening.

This lack of self-awareness in the ego experience, as it's happening, is what gives rise to the suffering that goes along with the ego experience. For example, right as this innovative form is beginning to take shape securely in the mind, there is no room for others in that state of mind. The deeper the egoic state of consciousness is, the deeper the selfishness is.

If your child comes up to you and asks you for help with their homework, you will not be present enough to stop what you're doing and help them. You are so deeply focused on the mind that you simply can't be bothered at an important time like this. You push them away for the time being, not giving any thought to how the rejection has caused suffering in the child.

The same goes for a husband or wife who requires some assistance or attention from you when you are busy being creative. You are so lost in the form this progression of the mind is taking that you just can't break away for even a minute for fear that you might lose the creativity if you lose your focus.

Ultimately, you will find that the more present you are, the more creativity has a chance to arise.

The opposite of this example would be if you were extremely self-aware and fully present in the moment. You would not be lost in the ego experience, nor would you have any desire to selfishly cause suffering to others. You are witnessing the beauty in the unfolding of the mind, yet you are not lost in it.

When this happens and you are fully present, there is no deep attachment to thoughts of the future. No fears that something will be lost if you stop what you are doing to be present for someone else.

The beauty of being fully present at all times is the freedom that comes with true self-awareness. There is no egoic "me" that needs to create anything. There is only the freedom and space that full consciousness offers us that requires no doing or creating. The present moment is perfect and complete and requires nothing from your ego to remain that way. Nothing is added to the present moment, and nothing can be taken away.

This state of being is free from all human suffering and allows you the opportunity to be present for others to help end their suffering.

Chapter 17

OPPOSITES

Opposites only exist in the mind/body experience and can be seen everywhere in all things from waking up in the morning to going to bed at night, from the sun rising to the sun setting, even day and night are opposites, love and hate, etc. The mind is constantly dominated by opposites in the form of thoughts and concepts.

These concepts are what the ego bases its reality on. They are fashioned together over the years by what we label as experiences, and the total of both good and bad experiences is what we consider ourselves to be. The storyline of me plays out in a world where opposites can exist and not only exist but can be considered completely real. This is where the separation occurs once again from your true self-awareness, back to the ego-self. When self-awareness disappears or living in the moment ceases, opposites creep back in and dominate the mind/body experience and your awareness shrinks from enjoying presence to witnessing opposing extremes of the mind.

When self-awareness or just simply the presence of being one with this moment has subsided, the door is left wide open for the ego or false self to flood back into your awareness. When this happens, all the things that exist in the illusion of the ego are made possible and seem to be absolutely real. The simplicity and peacefulness of the present moment are now gone, and the ego allows opposites to be experienced. When stuck in this state of consciousness, life can seem like a never-ending roller coaster ride.

These opposing forces that are constantly in play in the mind are what give rise to the illusion that you can choose who or what you want to become in life. It gives rise to the notion that what you are experiencing in the world of form is all there is. It is that place in the mind where you can find mental absolutes. Unfortunately, mental absolutes are ultimately narrow-mindedness and basically, you have a mental fixation on a single concept. There is no room left in your awareness to witness anything other than a single thought or solution to a situation.

The most common experience is when you are verbally or physically attacked, and the absolute only solution is to attack the other person back. Sadly, these types of illusions cause the most human suffering, and you hardly ever return to the present moment until after it happens or if it is a really strong emotion until you are sitting in jail or sitting in the hospital thinking to yourself that you wished you would have just walked away.

This is why trying to gain some self-awareness in your life can be the most important decision you ever make and one that can keep you on a peaceful path your entire life where you never have to experience horrible, unbridled reactive extremes of the ego. If you ever find yourself in this type of situation, meditate on how it all played out.

These types of opposites only serve as a helpful pointer to remind you that when you see no possible way out of a situation you could be stuck in the mind-dominated state of consciousness.

When those types of situations arise, the best thing to do is absolutely nothing. Just stay non-reactive and watch your self-awareness return, which creates the space for the mental absolute to subside.

Another common mental absolute is when you feel you have to change your life. The only way one illusion is replaced by another is when the clinging to one extreme is relinquished, which allows the mind the freedom to swing back to the opposing extreme. Most people call this choosing a better path in life, but really, they have just taken a thought that they used to consider good and labeled it bad. When one way of living is not working any longer, it is released mentally because your ego no longer wishes to be identified with it. When this happens, it allows for the opposite thought to be witnessed that is now considered better, at which time your ego clings to the new thought it deems as good. This is how new illusions are born! Egoic life is a constant series of trading one illusion for another. One moment you are single, the next you are in a relationship. One moment you don't have children, and then the next moment you do. Another moment you are renting, and the next you are buying a house. The list of opposites and egoic illusions is endless, which is why you can stay lost chasing down different ones your entire life and never truly find the root of your consciousness.

An easy example to understand would be any habit that you used to do daily, such as smoking or drinking. At one time, you considered those habits good and fun, and they made you happy, but eventually, when the mental attachment to such thoughts begins to weaken, they no longer serve your ego a purpose. Your ego then considers the change to be major, and it strengthens your mental attachment to the new form you are finding in your sense of self. Ultimately, once again, neither good thought nor bad thought is real; both are the same thing taking on different forms. The only thing that ever truly changes is your willingness to accept one form and deny the other. You can lose yourself in either thought and never truly be found, which is why the mental struggle for your happiness can go on forever and take on a multitude of different forms.

Most people call these major forms jobs, relationships, friendships, addictions, or anything that you find a sense of self in. In essence, the illusions in the storyline change, but you are no closer to finding your true self because you are searching in all the wrong places. You don't become a better person just because your ego simply changes forms and labels it better. You can buy a huge house and fancy things and surround yourself with all the materialistic forms that uphold the illusion that you are doing great in life, yet you are still free to choose to murder somebody tomorrow. Ask yourself, how is this possible if you are such a "better person" based on thought and outward action and you will see that life is just a series of illusions built on another until a solid sense of self is experienced and considered reality.

Ultimately, the mind can manipulate and fashion any storyline it chooses to uphold the illusion of the ego, but because the reality is that the storyline of any form is simply another illusion, it always gives you the freedom to choose something different at any time. You can spend sixty years being the greatest person the world has ever known, and you can surround yourself with millions of people who think the same thing, and on your sixty-first birthday, you kill somebody out of anger. Does the world still think you are a great person? Do you still think there is any true eternal reality to the illusion of greatness, or would you have had to die the day before your sixty-first birthday to maintain that illusion or storyline of greatness for the world? The biggest problem with these mental storylines is that any storyline can be shattered instantly by experiencing the opposite.

Do you think you are a cop and will always and forever be a cop? Do you think you are a firefighter? If you start a fire or commit a crime, you will see the storyline maintains the illusion, but only as long as you continue to stay within the parameters of the mental concept.

Another example could be when the concept of love occurs in the mind, and you're completely dominated by it. Have you ever noticed how it seemed real at the time like it would last forever? You witness not only conceptualized love in the mind but also feelings in the body that accompany the arising thoughts. As we all know, this type of love that exists in the mind has an opposite, and we call this falling out of love, or being heartbroken. The ego has lost something it was clinging to and not by choice either.

The question here is if love was considered real, then where did the love go? This thought form has taken the shape of true love, and true love is supposed to last forever. So how did it disappear? You need to ask yourself, how can something that is made to be real in the mind not last forever? How can this hugely amazing love affair be so ultimately conditional in the end? How can the very loving reasons that brought two people together ultimately have opposite reasons for tearing them apart?

The simple fact is that the love that you thought was real came from the mind, and it only proves that what goes up also can come back down. The mind works like this: thought forms arise and your ego either clings to them mentally at which point it creates your reality, or you do not cling to the thought, and it subsides at which point it just remains another passing thought.

Ultimately, this is why conceptualized love can always have a time limit on it. The length of time, as we all know from experiences, will only depend on the amount of time that both people are willing to work at holding the illusion firmly in their awareness. Once either person stops clinging to the illusion, the illusion of mental love subsides, and they choose to go their own way.

Unconditional love is the only type of love that has no opposite. It has room for the two opposing extremes of the mind, and anything contained within those extremes to arise and subside without placing any egoic judgment. Unconditional love comes from a place of true self-awareness. It comes from the understanding of what it truly means to live in the present moment. Unconditional love doesn't carry along with it mistakes from the past, or fears of the future. It does not keep track of rights or wrongs. It is not harmed at all or altered by the actions of others, for it does not depend on such things to exist.

Unconditional love is the stillness of the mind, it is an awareness of the recognition that you both have sometimes extreme differences, but you are both in the same human struggle. It gives other people the freedom to be themselves without fear that they will eventually screw up so badly that they will no longer be loved.

Unconditional love can't be offered to situations of the past or the future. You can't just look back and say I forgive you for cheating on me and call that unconditional love and expect that forgiveness to last forever as that is just mental acceptance of a negative event and you will on some level continue to struggle with it for the rest of the relationship, because everything in the mind is interconnected. You can't pluck out one event where betrayal was experienced and say I forgive you for betraying our relationship because it wasn't just betrayal that was experienced. It was anger, loss of trust, jealousy, and a multitude of other interconnected parts of the relationship that were affected, and every time you run into just one of those issues, it will always trigger trauma from the event. That trauma is the storyline you continue to drag around with you and your unwillingness to let it go is what causes the suffering! There were probably lots of wonderful things that happened in the past, but your ego mostly clings to bad experiences when the pain arises. That is why a storyline has no use in the present moment. The arising pain was a pointer that you were clinging so tightly to a concept at the time that there was no freedom to allow an event to arise and subside without experiencing something negative. This is why it is so important to offer yourself forgiveness because the other person was just working from their ego as well; they were probably completely unaware of anything, but their selfishness at the time.

The kind of forgiveness you need to be seeking exists in the present moment, where your ego no longer carries the negative storyline. If you no longer cling to the past, then there is truly nothing to forgive. You are accepting the present moment perfectly as it is without the egoic need to change anything to make it more perfect in your mind.

This is why unconditional love doesn't exist in the mind because it has to be experienced now in the present moment. It has to be offered right now as a new argument arises, or as the other person does something that you dislike. Unconditional love offers you the opportunity to love an imperfect person perfectly. It will stand the test of time if both people can offer it. Otherwise, one person will always reach a breaking point if they are working from mental love because anything that exists in the mind has a beginning and an end, which means that there is a comfort zone and a breaking point.

This is sadly why the ego keeps a record of all the rights and wrongs and bases its love on it accordingly. If you were to ask a person who practices unconditional love for many examples of when their partner screwed up last, they probably wouldn't be able to come up with very many examples as they do not retain the awareness of such events. They experience freedom from the storyline.

On the other hand, if the other person is working from egoic love, then they can probably recall hundreds of examples of their partner screwing up. Their life is experienced as one big storyline of events. Their ego clings tightly to it and they would, quite honestly, be lost without it. How can they remain right in their mind without PROOF or examples of the other person screwing up? Sadly, this is the reason why you rarely see any couple stand the test of time. One of them usually cannot give up the storyline long enough to ever experience true, unconditional love. They always need to be somehow better than the other person. To them, the relationship is usually all about the mental position. It is about what they are doing right and what the other person is doing wrong. They are working harder and contributing more to the relationship than the other person because they believe what they are doing now is eternal and it will always be like that. They have no true concept of the arising and subsiding of experiences and no true awareness that we live in a world of constant change. If the other person ever challenges that concept of rightness, then big trouble ensues. Remember, the ego will fight to the death to remain right, but luckily death only comes in the form of a relationship.

If both parties want to experience unconditional love, then they both need to seek out a deep appreciation for the other person and each other's struggles. You need to give up the egoic pull to constantly drag the past into the present moment as ammunition in an attempt to prove yourself right in an argument, and you need to allow the arising negative thoughts and experiences to subside without the need to cling to them. I'm sure it sounds like a lot of work as most relationships are experienced as constant battles, but one person with self-awareness will always seek peace, while the other constantly seeks battle. Two people with self-awareness will rarely find the need to argue or ever lose their peace and harmony because the selfishness of the ego no longer dominates their awareness. They are quick to forgive and always try to be understanding because they realize that the anger is coming from their attachment to their ego and that no true feelings can be hurt by anything the other person does. They have lots of space for bad things to arise and they will always try to do right by the other person when it comes down to it. They do not experience selfishness on the same level as a person working from ego. Remember that everybody has moments of presence or compassion all the time. It is the ones who need chaos most of the time to feel like solving that chaos is what gives their mind a sense of importance. They feel like they have added a new layer to the relationship when they have just continued to exist in different forms of the mind and have completely missed the peace the present moment always offers.

A true unconditional and loving relationship can be the most rewarding type. It offers you ultimate freedom in the relationship. You don't need to constantly struggle to maintain the idea that your relationship needs to fit neatly into the egoic shoebox that you have created for it in your mind. You don't need to do all things out of the fear that if you do not work every second of every day to create amazing experiences, your relationship will end. It gives you the freedom to allow the relationship to expand and contract when needed and also gives you freedom from fear.

You are experiencing life in the present moment, and you are no longer clinging to any egoic ideas about how you need to control the other person to feel secure. You can offer them the best parts of yourself effortlessly without any mental attachments to the continuation of a pleasant storyline and you no longer will feel a need to punish them if they do something you don't agree with. You will always greet them with open arms because your inner peace does not depend on anything outward.

Living a life free of extreme opposites in any form is probably why you are searching for self-awareness in the first place. It is a worthy search and one that has peace as a result. Once you understand the opposing extremes of the mind, you never need to get lost in either of them again. You can still have lots of nice things in life, but you will find that the reasons for them completely change. It is not what you have that makes you peaceful; it is your willingness to accept the present moment in any form that allows you to experience peace. Ask yourself if you would still be peaceful and feel secure if all of your nice things were suddenly taken away. The ego wants to believe that you would remain peaceful, but the reality is most people would rather die than lose all the things that they think they attained in life. Once again, mental attachment is what creates suffering, whether it is with people or possessions or thoughts or feelings!

Chapter 18

3 CONCEPTS OF THE MIND

I will give three simple concepts of the mind. The first one is the concept of a parent. A pregnancy occurs, which opens the doors for all kinds of other thoughts to flood into the mind. Now you're questioning whether you are truly ready for kids or if you will be a good parent, or if you are willing to sacrifice your freedom to take on this concept of what a good parent would be. We all know that to be a good parent you have to be willing to live your life for another, which most people are not fully willing to do because of selfishness.

Now one concept, such as being a parent at one point in your life, has a ton of concepts attached to it, and in the process, your self-awareness has shrunk and now your ego-self has grown. You now have the egoic potential to live out the rest of your life trying to play the role of a good parent, and your entire life focus could now be shrunk to this single ego-defining concept. Self-awareness is awareness of this present moment, and most parents are stuck in thoughts of the past about how their life could have been or thoughts of the future when they regain a sense of freedom after the kids are grown. When this happens the life, you have at this exact moment passes you by and you might end up living in regret when it's all said and done looking back and thinking what might have been if you were just self-aware and present all the time with your children instead of being stuck playing the role of a parent or a good provider.

The second concept is that of a scientist. You are highly educated in the ways of the mind even to the point of being considered a genius. You could very well spend your entire life trying to prove that you are a great scientist by challenging other mental theories or doing ground-breaking work in a certain field of your choosing or even pushing the limits of the known scientific universe. Your entire awareness could be consumed with how you define yourself as a scientist and how it's up to you to change or possibly save the world. This concept is great, but self-awareness is now so limited that this ego awareness of how you define yourself is in control of your life. Even the easiest things in life might start to seem impossible. Your ego could be so heavily in control that you are so far to one extreme searching the outer edges of the mind that you might have forgotten what it was like to be a good husband or a good wife. You might have forgotten that your child's life is passing you by and they may never get to really know you. You might not be able to see what this passion for science is doing to the people who love you the most. You could be caring so much about the concepts of the mind that you could be willing to spend all of your time in a laboratory. You could end up possibly losing your family because you no longer are present for them. It seems hard to keep a marriage healthy when you experience this enormous sense of importance to your work at the same time.

Self-awareness is awareness of this present moment without adding anything to it, and most scientists are stuck in thoughts of the future or even looking for answers in the past of what other scientists before them have done. The life they could have passed them by all to attain a few new thoughts or concepts to share with the world. Luckily, it's possible to be a scientist and live very simply in this moment with those who love you the most and still make great contributions to science.

The third concept is that of a spiritual seeker. Most people who begin a spiritual search either are sick of denying the present moment or meet a spiritual guru. They might try to read books from a spiritual guru. To most people, a spiritual guru is someone who has a high sense of awareness, or possibly a person with some type of spiritual ability that you believe you don't possess. This spiritual search now follows the path of whatever concept you have of spirituality.

You could start reading books or seek out a teacher who wears the right spiritual clothing. A teacher could burn incense and set up a very peaceful meditation space. They could have pictures of their teacher on the wall with lineage going back many generations and give all of their credit to their mentor who came before them. You could have spiritual experiences and gain tons and tons of spiritual information. You might witness some psychic abilities, and you are now reading auras and channeling the spirit world, reading tarot, or developing healing abilities. It might feel wonderful like you are starting to become a spiritual person. The problem now arises that all of these things fit perfectly into your concept of spirituality and what you believe a spiritual life is like. You now begin to take on all the qualities of a spiritual person based on all the concepts that are being attained through spiritual investigation, and no matter what anybody has to say about it, you are now a spiritual being sharing human experiences.

The ego-self is still fully in place at this point, but you won't know it because you believe all the spiritual experiences you have had that you can't explain simply prove that you are now becoming spiritual. The ego-self could trick you into believing you need to move to Tibet, shave your head, and live the rest of your life in meditation in a cave.

Unfortunately, true self-awareness is awareness of this present moment, and it can be experienced anywhere in the world without needing anything of form. There is no perfect place for self-awareness; it doesn't require anything to be experienced. Self-awareness itself is the perfection and self-mastery that you seek.

The unattainable concept of perfection that exists in the mind however is always sought out in one form or another because in the mind there is always something more that needs to be added to the belief structure that your ego is attempting to build. You might believe that the foundation of your spiritual enlightenment lies in relocating to some sacred place where you believe the most enlightened people live. Now that you have moved there you look around and realize you need to dress differently to fit in. So, you put on the same type of clothes as everyone else. Now things are going pretty well, and you feel like you are making progress so next you learn how to chant, and you spend hours a day chanting in a group with all the other spiritual seekers. Next, you learn to sit and meditate for countless hours. You begin a process of treating people more gently, and you soften your tone of voice. You might vow to become a vegetarian and practice compassion for all beings. The list is endless, but now you have painted a pretty picture in your mind, and you start a daily routine that allows you to believe that you are super spiritual now and that life is great, and that you have come so far from where you started.

The problem is once you leave your little community of like-minded people and return to the daily grind of your life back home, nobody else is going to help maintain the illusion that you are a spiritual person. You might begin to struggle with everyday interactions with what you consider nonspiritual people. You might begin to feel the happiness you had been experiencing back in your sacred place diminish. In an attempt to solidify your spirituality, your ego might lead you to believe that you just shouldn't surround yourself with your old friends or family or anybody who begins to challenge your new beliefs.

You might begin to believe that they simply are not on your level or that there is no longer a benefit in knowing them. All of this spiritual work you have done has now caused a separation where you only want to surround yourself with other spiritual seekers. If self-awareness is completely gone, you might even develop a type of cult mentality where your beliefs are right and everyone else is wrong to the point that you can't even entertain the beliefs of another person or have even a slight bit of willingness to attempt to understand where they are coming from. Your ego just puts you up on a pedestal and your beliefs reign supreme. That is how scary any type of religious or spiritual search can be if left unchecked; it can get out of hand and cause not only yourself but others, tremendous suffering.

Sometimes when important beliefs such as religion or spirituality are challenged, the ego will fight to a literal death with any other person if the challenge is strong enough.

You have to be very careful not to follow anything outward in your search, but to turn inward for all of your answers. I could have ended up in a cave in Tibet if self-realization never happened to me when it did. I had wanted to take the spiritual trip of a lifetime as well. Luckily, I'm blessed to be able to have cultivated self-awareness here among my family and friends. I think the only benefit you will find by undergoing such an extreme search is maybe you will be freer from everyday big city distractions in Tibet, but hopefully, by sharing these things in this book, you'll see that it's possible to find the same things here living a busy life at home.

You might see how through these examples it is easy to stay stuck living out the ego-self or lost in the mind altogether, never really ever present in this very moment able to surround yourself with all types of people no matter what form their ego has taken. Those were only three examples of the ego experience. Now imagine how many other roles the ego experience can take on to define your false limited sense of self. To cultivate inner self-awareness of the present moment is the only thing you need to do to become a spiritual person. To live fully in this moment and touch this life very deeply is to truly live a divine existence. Start cultivating self-mastery in whatever you do so that unconditional love and compassion for all others have the chance to shine through to the surface instead of all the limiting and negative things that the shrunken ego attempts to cling to as reality that can cause not only separation from the present moment but all other people as well.

Chapter 19

DESIRE

In the mind/body experience, the saying great minds think alike holds. In a deeper awareness of the self, the opposite is true, and the mind is transcended altogether for it no longer is considered to be "me" and only continues to serve up pointers to that realization.

In the mind/body experience, desire is one of the most frequently arising thought forms. It is the aspect of the ego that seeks to reward oneself for all the hard mental or physical work each of us experiences daily. Desire usually arises after spending the day trading away our hours for dollars at a job. Once you get off work you naturally want to seek out a more pleasurable experience.

Desire can manifest in the form of drugs, alcohol, sex, food, fun, or anything that feels like some type of reward.

Desire or that mental yearning will always pull you away from the present moment no matter what form it takes. Desire can be simple things like the attention from others even if you only desire hanging out with a group of friends or family. Desire is by far the most widely experienced obstacle in the spiritual path, because of how little attention is paid to self-awareness at the moment desire is manifesting or arising in whatever form it takes. The need for something better is the bread and butter of the ego experience. It can easily overtake your awareness and you won't know it until after you have gained that which you desired, and your strong ego-dominated awareness subsides.

To start with, explore the desires of drugs and alcohol. The tricky thing about them both is they fully ground you in the mind and body and take you as far away from the awareness of your true self as possible. A lot of people seek themselves in these two activities and it is easily mistaken to be true happiness because of the mental high, but every high has a low. Instead of bouncing back and forth between extremes, peace is the middle path where you want to be. The mind/body experience, such as thoughts, feelings, and emotions, when mixed can result in a deeply rooted mind-dominated state of consciousness through substance abuse.

People can spend an entire lifetime believing they have found themselves in the use of drugs or alcohol. When you are high or drunk, all of the ego senses and pleasures dominate your awareness. The ego is being fed by the concept of needing to add more to make life a better experience. It's the overwhelming feelings and sensations that make you feel like you are living life at the moment. It's usually a seductive experience. It can be a never-ending cycle of suffering by attempting to find oneself in the stimulation of the mind and body. In the end, you usually just end up creating suffering for yourself and those around you as your selfishness attempts to gorge itself on whatever substance you have your hands on at the time.

The reason people can get so lost chasing down the next high is they are completely lost in the mind-dominated state of consciousness. Life becomes all about adding more to the present moment at any cost. They are stuck in a pleasure-seeking mental maze, naively believing that they can sustain some sort of happiness or pleasure if they just remain high or drunk. They get locked in a vicious cycle of chasing down one failed attempt at eternal happiness after another; all the while unaware that mental happiness depends on something of form to sustain itself. When you are living in this mind-dominated state you don't realize that suffering is masking itself in a form of something desirable. You think that by chasing the next high you can actually return to a state of peace, but it's just one gigantic illusion, and the happiness comes and goes just as quickly as the high does which lets you know that it wasn't true happiness at all.

The ego is built on desire; it is one of the hardest illusions to see through. Desire for the ego is like oxygen to the body, you simply can't exist without it. If you spent your entire life creating every day solely based on fulfilling your desires in one form or another, how would you even know where to begin looking for the root of it? This is a very important question to ask and probably the beginning of true self-awareness arising in your life if you are curious about it. You need to pay very close attention to every reaction your mind instantly has to arising thought forms. Slowly bring awareness to every desire as it arises to question why you do the things you do. When you practice this enough and dig deep, you will see that your storyline begins to unfold itself for you. Hopefully, you will begin to see that you don't know why you do anything, and the awareness will arise that it's something that you have always done. Hopefully, as more self-awareness continues to arise for you, the process will have you question everything that you have taken for granted. You will start to look at why you say the things you do and why you treat certain people the way you do. You become aware that all of your habits are mental attachments to routines and illusions based on storylines. It is mental attachments that produce the most suffering, which is why it is so important to bring awareness to them.

Truly questioning all desires as they arise will eventually lead to challenging some of the deepest beliefs that your ego holds dear. You need to prepare yourself for the possibility that this new awareness will create some instability in your life. When some major illusions crumble, you might begin to feel lost, but luckily as with all things in the mind/body experience, it is only a matter of time before those thoughts change and you can begin to adapt to the new awareness that you are allowing to arise in the present moment. It is important to have awareness both of the thoughts that arise and subside in the mind, but also of the nothingness before the thoughts ever arise. That is where your freedom from the ego exists. That is the space that is true inner peace.

The ego has no awareness of this space, nor does it want awareness of it. The ego defines itself only by the thoughts that you stack on top of one another and the experiences you cling to that create your storyline.

Chapter 20

PEOPLE DON'T CHANGE

WHEN YOU ARE FIRMLY ROOTED in the egoic experience, you fail to see the fact that the people around you don't ever truly change. The only thing that is in constant change is your ability to witness the changing forms of the mind as they arise and subside.

Outwardly, there may be a million different forms arising and subsiding with each individual that the ego could consider this change. Your ego would label it either by saying that the person is slowly progressing toward becoming a better person, or slowly declining and sinking into the pits of depression and degradation. You might think that they are either becoming a productive member of society or a social outcast. You might also unknowingly place a certain level of worth on each individual depending on his or her social status. Keep in mind that these beliefs only take place in the mind itself.

Your particular thoughts on the matter when continuing to carry out the separation between all human beings, have no real truth to it, because we are all equally important.

One can cling to one thought as it arises over another, based on a positive or negative mental outlook at the time the thought is witnessed. You can be upset one day and make all kinds of negative thoughts simply by having a heavy attachment to the ego at the moment. On the flip side, you can be mentally free, feel great, and have a happy positive outlook about yourself and others as well. The world around you doesn't necessarily change the way you think it does, only your ability to be present enough to view your arising and subsiding thoughts about it changes.

You can see the thought arising that has the potential to lead you to believe that the person is progressing in their life based on adding one more thing of form to your egoic concept of them, such as they just started college. By adding the thought form that college makes you a better person, you have now shifted your mental perspective of who you think they are without any true change happening.

If you add a negative thought form, such as that person just went to jail. Ask yourself how you would describe that person. How is that person's ego described based on your own beliefs about how you view jail? Can you now see that the person hasn't changed at the core of their being? Only your thoughts about them have changed based on your views and opinions of the egoic separation that takes place between humans when viewing the world from the mind-dominated state of consciousness. Your thoughts are usually based on how you are doing in life as a comparison. What if you have been to jail and came out of it thinking you were a better person, would you still view a person in jail as a complete hopeless failure?

The ego bases its structure on outward things of form to secure its inward position in this world. If one outward form is deemed positive, then an addition to the ego-self is made. If the outward form is negative, then a subtraction of the mental self-worth is taken away. This process of adding and subtracting only exists in the mind. When you're lost in mental forms like this, how could you possibly know your true self? How could you possibly touch the present moment deeply, if you are busy doing math in your mind? If you are busy making judgments and assumptions about other people based on your thoughts about yourself and what you are doing with your life, then how can you possibly see others for what they truly are?

The ego will keep you constantly on the search for who you are. Only when true self-awareness is present, does this egoic search end, and the allowance of the present moment's peacefulness of accepting all forms of life as one begins.

Ultimately, you or any other person on earth never truly changes. The consciousness that allows the world of form to be experienced is the only constant you will ever know.

Consciousness is the unifying factor that makes every single person on earth the same; it only takes on different forms. Luckily, consciousness needs no distinction between different forms because we are all equals.

You could have been born on the opposite side of the world, but you and I are only different in the form that has arisen in the mind/body experience. The driving factor that gives rise to the ability to witness the world of form is ultimately what you are, and it can only be found in the present moment. Don't get lost in the mind chasing down one mental form after another stuck in an endless cycle of finding the same thing in a different form. Only when you give up the need for change or the desire to find out who you are, do you let go enough mentally to touch the present moment and realize you have always been the very thing you have always searched for. Below the surface of the mind, you are and forever will be at eternal peace.

Chapter 21

GLORIFIED EGO

Your best bet for seeing the glorified ego experience for what it is without knowing a famous person or being a movie star would be to think back to high school. The heightened ego experience was in full swing, and all these extra illusions were being added to the thought of ME, HIM, or HER because of a person's popularity or perception. The main characters in the storyline of high school were built up to the point of fame for some kids. Everybody wanted to be like them and have the same experiences, friends, cars, or clothes. The popular kids were kings and queens of the school.

Sadly, as life goes on and the ego illusions are not kept up any longer by all the people who bought into them, the fame and glory fade, and most just return to the thought of regular people as life continues. The group consciousness of the school that once held all these illusions firmly in place splits up after graduation and everyone ventures to strike out on their own.

They get a job or have some kids, and the glory days are now reduced to what people would call normal life experiences shared by a few families and friends.

The high-school sweethearts that stayed together after high school and ended up married usually have problems down the road at a certain point when the diminished ego can no longer be tolerated, and you begin to hear things like you were so much better back in high school and now look at you. If continued outward success after high school isn't experienced, problems arise. The selfish egoic thoughts of what I deserve or desire out of life now come into play, and if a person's ego isn't being fed what it craves based on the illusions the particular person holds in their mind, then all kinds of things can arise such as fear, anger, greed, frustration, anxiety, low self-esteem, depression, the list is endless. Life is not being lived in the moment and suffering occurs because getting by is simply not good enough for the inflated ego. Any type of person that experiences this simply needs to give up the storyline that they were a great person and somehow that dropped off. Nothing has truly changed, only the fact that you are no longer surrounded by lots of people who helped maintain that illusion is no longer present.

Chapter 22

WINNING AND THE EGO

THE EGO HAS a constant need to win, no matter what form it takes on. The less attachment to doing better or being better is a sign that you are not as heavily attached to that aspect of the ego as others could be. You can look around you at all times and see the people that must win or be better than others at all costs. This winning could take the form of an argument, a contest that only exists in the mind such as who is more fashionable, or who is more popular. It takes the form of who has a nicer car or a better job or a bigger house. Usually, the thoughts about who has more money or more possessions can keep the attachment to the ego alive and on its quest for financial domination and separation from others until retirement or even death. This mentality is about progressing while proving you have a better life by buying nice things.

This constant desire to be slightly better or slightly different than everybody else around you is the very attachment to the ego that continues to produce the separation between all humans. If you are busy chasing down your egoic dreams, then how can you possibly be present to help others? The concept of no two people existing on earth exactly the same is what drives this attachment to the ego that we all have. People just look around with their eyes and never with true self-awareness. The mind only sees differences everywhere it looks, which is why everybody wants to somehow be unique. You have all seen or heard about some famous person on the red carpet who has an absolute fit and feels completely embarrassed when they realize another famous person showed up to the same event wearing the same outfit. They proudly walked the red carpet thinking the moment was a giant win because they had what they considered the best dress on and all of a sudden it became a failure when they realized they weren't the only one in that dress.

So many people are consumed with the thought of having more or being more than others that they simply forget what it means to have compassion for others. Their super-inflated ego is so heavily focused on winning everything they come across that they are stuck in the progression of the mind which leaves the door wide open for huge swings in emotions to be experienced.

Their selfishness dominates their human experience and life is all about what they want when they want it.

Sadly, a lot of people with no self-awareness would consider this type of life a huge win, but you will only experience mental peace and happiness as long as you can keep spending money to maintain the illusion of outward happiness.

The moment the money runs out or the fame ends is usually when a heavy depression sets in. You could spend the rest of your life constantly clinging to the past and what you had and completely miss the peace and freedom that the present moment can offer you today.

Chapter 23

CHOOSE YOUR FORM

THE BEST THING about being able to experience the world of form is the numerous choices we have. We can choose to experience the softer side of form like gardening, singing, meditating, or things that don't have the potential to create suffering. Or we can go to the other extreme and choose to dabble in forms like fighting a war, skydiving, drag racing, or extreme mountain climbing. A good rule of thumb is the more intense the form, the more potential that it has to kill you or others.

I like using fishing as an example because we have all probably been fishing at least once in our lifetime. The simplest form of fishing is sitting on the shore of a lake and casting your fishing line out into the water. Now when you begin the egoic process of needing more, wanting more, or having more, you obviously begin adding more things of form to get the desired results.

When fishing from the shore is no longer good enough, you now add a boat. Instead of peacefully living in the present moment, sitting on the shore fishing not caring one way or another if you catch any fish or not, you are now out in the middle of the lake in a boat. Just by adding one more thing of form, the potential danger has increased substantially. The possibility of drowning or wrecking your boat can now arise simply by the desire to find yourself by going deeper into the form of fishing. You want to catch more fish, you want to catch bigger fish, and you've always grown up believing this can only happen by doing things the right way. So now you must research the form of fishing. You believe you must now do your homework to become a better fisherman. This whole process of "doing" is what takes you deeper into the ego experience.

As you begin to have more and more experiences with the form of fishing, you begin a process of defining yourself as a fisherman. You are now becoming lost in the form of fishing because you mistakenly believe that you are finding yourself by doing the actual fishing and catching the biggest and best fish. The ego always has a sense of progression, and now you are adding all the right fishing gear, and you now have the nice truck and fishing boat. You now believe that by all this doing and all this adding to the thought of yourself, you have found that place of peace and talent inside yourself on the lake that you aren't able to find anywhere else.

When you get this deeply focused on any outward activity, you can take any form to the point of being considered a professional. The problem is now that the form of fishing has become the biggest thing in your life, and you define yourself as a fisherman, the moment you take away the boat and the lake and the fish, suffering occurs.

Hopefully, now you can see how easy it is to get lost in any form. The form can always be something different. You can look deeply into the form of basketball and mistakenly believe you have found yourself there, but ultimately you are doing the same thing as fishing, it has just taken on a different form. You are still lost searching for yourself in the mind. If you weren't able to define yourself as the thing you love the most like a fisherman or a basketball player, who would you be if the form of fishing or basketball were taken away? You only know you are truly found when you don't require anything of form to define yourself.

You also have to be careful of how similar forms can appear but can ultimately be completely different. For example, let's say you wish to attend a peace rally. You show up at this rally and surround yourself with other like-minded people who are seeking and enjoying peace.

This would be a wonderful event to attend, and it would probably make you feel really good about yourself.

Now let's say you were to attend an anti-war rally. It might seem like the same thing mentally, but it could be completely different. You could attend a rally promoted by people whose egos are anything but peaceful. Their conceptualized views on war might lead them to be angry, and even though they want the war to end to promote peace, they might allow their angry egos to say things that do not promote peace. You could get a little lost in that type of gathering and leave that rally with the potential of feeling anger towards war as well. As you can see, they are both similar concepts, with the potential of having two completely different outcomes.

When you are high or drunk, the world of form slowly melts away until your worldview is shrunk to only the perception of what is going on with your ego-self or what you want or think you are getting at the time. Along with those things, all the responsibilities of the world temporarily melt away and your awareness is fully aligned with the ego-self and extreme selfishness is the resulting experience in that moment. Can you see the tricky thing in that realization? True self-awareness is the realization that the only thing that exists is consciousness, and the self-awareness experienced in the ego uses everything of form to create the illusion that you exist purely in the moment and being your true self. You are not because instead of giving everything up, you clung to every single illusion possible until you thought you experienced true freedom. This is also the difference between true enlightenment and the conceptualized enlightenment of the mind only. The reason this is a trick is because, at that moment, your mind believes that not only is it getting exactly everything it wants, but also that things like the suffering of the past are gone, including fears of the future, the worries of paying bills on time, and it covers up the thought of someone who died or is dying. There are no limits to what the mind believes is being covered up with this moment of fun or pleasure-seeking. The only way for that suffering to truly end is to see through the ego-self and to let full self-awareness shine through in its place, hence the biggest trick or obstacle in the spiritual path. It always holds true that when you're stuck in the ego-self or false self you are getting the extreme opposite of that which you truly seek.

This is how cheating on someone you love manifests in the moment of fully being stuck in the ego-self. The only thing that matters is the concept of YOU, and your true self-awareness that has guarded and protected the concept of a relationship with another was washed away by pure selfishness. I think all people, whether they know it consciously or subconsciously, know exactly what they are, and we are all fighting to get home to that truth to experience that salvation and the end of suffering that the mind/body experience is built on. The problem is the road home is a minefield. With each step you take, if self-awareness and full attention are not paid to living in this present moment and touching it deeply and fully, the next step you take will be on a mine. It is then that your self-awareness completely blows up in your face, and you're once again grounded in the mind/body experience. Even after full self-realization happens, the ego still fights for survival, and moments of un-mindfulness constantly arise. If you are not aware that in the moment, you're witnessing your ego-self you too could find yourself in conflicts and drama that can still arise even to the enlightened person. Deep awareness in this moment must be paid and the practice of allowing the mind/body experience to exist as it is without clinging to any of it is the only way I know how to allow self-awareness to stay present more times than not.

Chapter 24

PRESENCE OF MIND

WHEN WAS the last time you got excited about life and just said yes to it no matter what form it took? When was the last time that you were free enough to experience the joy, peace, and happiness of the present moment? Most of us would try to remember back to the last time something we mentally label "good" happened and say, yes, that's it, that was the last time I was fully present because I experienced peace, joy, and happiness.

The problem is if you were to take away the good thing and replace it with something your mind would label bad, then you wouldn't call it peace, happiness, or joy at all. This is a good pointer to how unaware of the present moment most of us are.

You can't base your concept of presence on the outcome of a particular event, thought, or feeling. True presence isn't dependent on whether something is good or bad for the mind to be peaceful and happy.

The ego experience is the roller coaster that allows for these mental ups and downs to occur when things of an outward nature change for what the mind believes to be better or worse. The newness of a positive mental form that is arising is what gives birth to a new egoic attachment by adding something to it such as a new lover, or a new house, job, or car.

The outward transitions of form are what most of us base our inward thoughts and emotions on. For example, let's say that a new promotion at work suddenly became available, and your ego so desperately desires it that it is willing to do anything to get it.

As an outward attempt at performing your job duties to your fullest extent happens, you now push everything else in your life out of the picture for the time being and just solely focus on getting that promotion. In the mind at this point, nothing else matters. That is your sole desire, and you will bring a single-minded focus to achieve it. The selfish cycle of the ego is now doing what it always does, it is only chasing after a different form now. You are once again attempting to find yourself in this new promotion. You want to achieve it by saying, "This is the new me, look at all I have accomplished." The ego believes that only by constantly adding new and better additions to life's circumstances, does it make the thought of oneself bigger and better and more mentally secure.

The flip side of that mind-dominated state of consciousness is what if that promotion is given to someone else? What happens to you now at this point? The selfishness of the ego is no longer seeking to find itself in promotion; it has now begun to seek itself in depression and self-suffering. The promotion itself was just a mental form that the ego tried to add to itself, but because the ego was unsuccessful at adding the form of a promotion to itself, it naturally looks elsewhere for something new to add, even if it is suffering itself.

At this point, the inflated ego you witnessed as having this big promotion with a big pay raise slowly collapses and an awareness of a diminished ego is experienced. You were so deeply lost in thought about who or what the promotion would make you, that you completely lost the mental identity that you had currently held in place before the thought of a new promotion ever arose in your mind.

The suffering can take place because you let go of that egoic attachment to who you thought you were before the idea of a promotion. When times are mentally good, they are only good, because you have a firm egoic attachment set in place of who you believe you are at the time. The ego believes there is a "this" causing a "that," so because you worked so hard, you believed the promotion was yours. As you can see that isn't always the case, because "this" causing a "that" is just another illusion of the ego.

Whether you got the promotion and experienced peace, joy, and happiness, or you did not and experienced suffering and depression, now you can hopefully see that both examples exist in the mind only. No true presence was experienced while chasing after mental happiness or allowing mental unhappiness to occur. Once again, both are the same thing; they have just taken a different form. No true freedom from the ego was experienced while chasing happiness or allowing depression to take its place. This is the nature of witnessing the mind. You are only aware of the constantly changing mental states and have become lost in the forms they are taking. You are witnessing egoic thoughts of the future "you" that become better, or you are witnessing the future thoughts of the loss that "you" will not become better. You need to be willing to give up all egoic thoughts of the past or the future to have true experiences with the present moment. You need to be completely content with the present in any form it takes. You need to work backward through form. You need to keep removing what you think you are to experience the presence that is there before form ever has the chance to be witnessed.

Chapter 25

TRUE PRESENCE

As I EXPLAINED in the last chapter, if you are busy adding or subtracting thoughts to yourself then you will never touch the present moment deeply enough to experience freedom from all human suffering. The simple fact is that even if you did get a promotion and became happy, we all know that the happiness from the promotion never lasts forever. This simple observation points to the awareness that at some point when the happiness ends and the job is lost, suffering will once again occur.

The state of being that experiences the addition and subtraction to life is the illusion of the ego only. The ego experience demands progression, so you are busy either chasing after things that you desire or progressively avoiding things that you do not want to experience.

Consciousness has no opposite for it requires none. There is no form to it. Consciousness needs nothing to be added or subtracted to exist. The present moment is the closest thing in the mind/body experience that one might consider heaven. It is free from all the suffering in the world. It is the true presence of being.

The "YOU" that you are seeking to find in the world of form, is the very thing that keeps you completely unaware of the present moment itself. When you are trying so hard to make it in this life, you are just losing yourself deeper in the various forms that arise in the mind/body experience. It is only when you are willing to simply let go of being different, or separate from one another, can you find your way back to the present moment. It is the needs and desires of the ego that ultimately leave you feeling lost or alone in the world. Even if you have everything outwardly going for you, I bet inwardly there is still a void that no amount of love or fame or money or possessions can fill. People try so hard to cover up that void with outward things, yet at some point no matter how much they have, they will have a breakdown and the illusion of the ego will be seen through and the realization that all of it ultimately means nothing.

Having true presence or living in the present moment is the only possible way I know of to fill that void and end all human suffering. To be one with yourself or touch the present moment, you simply just exist without needing to change anything. The need to add something to make this moment better no longer arises; you have become one with yourself and one with all of mankind. The present moment is the only place to find true self-awareness. This is the only place to find what you might call enlightenment. Enlightenment is not something that twenty years of adding one spiritual form after another automatically unlocks. You could spend your entire life from birth till death drowning in spiritual forms and never truly touch the present moment.

Enlightenment is not about what you do, it is about unlocking your awareness of the formless state of presence. It is like saying, "I am," and stopping your mind before anything else follows those words. When you touch the present moment, you will understand that those two words are complete. They are a pointer to the state of being that experiences the present moment!

The present moment can't be found in any spiritual text because there is still a "you" and a "doing" that is taking place while reading. This is why ultimately in pursuit of the self all knowledge is completely useless other than to serve as a pointer to that which lies beyond the awareness of the mind-dominated state of consciousness. The present moment can't be read about; it can't be taught like a teacher can teach math. There is no progression to it. Nothing can be added to equal the present moment. You can't take a monastery full of monks plus incense plus meditation and equal the present moment.

The present moment can't be dug up in the form of some religious artifact from the earth that belonged to Jesus or Buddha. It can't be found in the world of form anywhere or in anything.

The present moment exists before all things of form ever have a chance to arise. You can sit in a monastery and be present, but if you lose yourself in the concept of being spiritual simply because of the monastic life itself, then you can waste your entire life there believing you are touching the present moment all the while you are only touching a peaceful secure mental state of mind. If you take away the peace and solidarity that the monastery provides, ask yourself if even the tiniest bit of suffering occurs. If so, then you have yet to gain a true understanding of the present moment or consciousness itself. True peace is existing perfectly in your life no matter what form it has taken without depending on anything outwardly to maintain the illusion.

The world of form is an incredibly tricky thing to gain awareness of when you are stuck in a mind-dominated state of consciousness. Ultimately if you are still stuck in the mind/body experience without any true self-awareness, then ultimately there is no difference between meditating in a monastery while believing you are spiritual or selling drugs to kids on the street while believing you're a big-time drug dealer. It's the same mind-dominated state of consciousness taking on different forms.

When true awareness of the present moment is experienced, you are no longer self-seeking in the world of form by locking yourself away in a monastery. You are now free to roam the world and help all others awaken no matter what form their ego experience has taken. The real gift of the present moment is the knowingness that the only differences that exist in this world exist in the mind only. We are all united through consciousness and we all can stop chasing the ego-self and help raise awareness through unconditional love and compassion for all others who are stuck in the ego experience. In the end, true presence is simply the ultimate awareness of the formless self, and it is not any more complicated or any less complicated than that.

Chapter 26

EGO AND WEIGHT LOSS

WHEN YOU ARE LIVING HEAVILY in the ego experience, you might fail to see that the only thing that is in constant motion is everything that is contained in the mind/body experience itself. There is no real motion to your consciousness unless you are witnessing the mind. When you are fully stuck in the mind, you experience thought after thought after thought arising and subsiding all the while reacting to every one of them like they are your reality. Most people fail to understand that if you no longer react to your thoughts, then there is no longer a reality to them. It is the doing-ness that creates the illusion of reality. What you say and attempt to act out is how your reality takes shape. You might witness a concept arising that if you eat less, you will lose weight when you should be aware that if you remain present you will always have a choice on what to eat, how much to eat, and when to eat it. You will no longer be ruled by the mind-dominated state that is constantly pleasure-seeking. If you were to spend one week off of your diet and one week on your diet, then you would see that the only thing that changes in yourself is your routine. Ultimately, the difference between the two opposing weeks is one week you were pleasure-seeking heavier, which could have resulted in weight gain. You were constantly trying to add more things of form to yourself and in this case, those things were food and drink. The pleasure-seeking is usually done without any true self-awareness present. This is how after ten years of pleasure-seeking using food, you all of a sudden one day look in the mirror and notice how overweight you are when you return to the present moment long enough to realize it.

We all know you don't gain weight by reading books and adding knowledge to the mind, so the form of pleasure-seeking physically by adding more food to your daily routine can simply be ended by bringing awareness to how unaware you are at the time you are eating. Try making your favorite dinner and take a few bites until your eyes roll back in your head from how delicious it is and then stop and put down the fork and ask yourself if you would be able to walk away from the rest of the meal for the rest of the night. If for any reason you are not, then it's a great pointer to the fact that you are trying to seek pleasure using food. The key to losing weight as always is awareness, for without awareness you are simply lost in the ego experience just following your habits and routines without giving any thought to them as they are happening. People who live in the present moment with their eating habits will usually view them as just one more daily routine to sit and be peaceful experiencing without worrying about what comes after. They are fully present and fully aware of their body and how it is reacting bite by bite. They know exactly the moment they are full and stop eating at which point they can fully move on to the next activity they had planned without ever looking back. When they notice hunger arising again, they can sit and be peaceful with the form of eating once again, but it does not dominate their awareness all day long.

People who are too far to one extreme of the ego experience will view their daily eating habits as a means to an end to reach a certain planned-out goal and will usually be focused on what goal they will move onto next during their meal. Eating to them is no longer a plea-sure-seeking experience, but more of an activity that needs to be gotten out of the way. A lot of people who experience eating this way will usually eat on the go and they place no real mental attachment to it other than it is just one more meal they got out of the way while staying on track.

The opposite extreme can occur when people have zero awareness of what they eat, as they are just pleasure-seeking at the time and eat whatever looks good. Some people call this grazing. It is when you constantly eat each time you witness thoughts about food arising in the mind. The trick to regaining control over your eating habits is you need to bring your full attention to what you are doing as you are doing it. It is called being present with your eating habits. If you are not present, then nobody is making choices for you as you are simply on autopilot and whatever you witness arising in the mind that seems most appealing at the time is the thing you will eat first. You tend to eat everything on your plate and don't experience being full because you eat so fast for the pleasure of it that the body no longer has time to catch up with how quickly you are eating the food. In this state of non-awareness, you might finish a full meal. Five minutes later you could be eating a bunch of desserts and then continue snacking on and off for the rest of the night.

The ego is a pleasure seeker at heart, and the bread and butter of the ego is its uncanny ability to continue to add things until you reach an extremely pleasurable mental creation. For example, you start with eating a healthy salad for lunch. First, you start with a nice bed of lettuce as your base. You then begin looking through your refrigerator, and instantly as something good catches your eye like lunch meat you reach for it and throw it on top of the lettuce. Then you see cheese and reach for it, but one kind might not be good enough, so you grab a few different kinds and mix them. Now, you have it loaded up with lettuce and lunch meat and cheeses. But wait, all of a sudden, some bacon bits you had stashed in your door catches your eye, so you sprinkle some of that on. Then you grab your dressing of choice and squeeze a bunch over the top. Now that you have a pretty good heap of stuff on there, you might remember that you have croutons in the cupboard, and right as you reach for croutons you might see sunflower seeds. I mean the list could be endless. You can spy a tomato in your crisper and throw that on there and might continue doing this all in the name of health until there isn't possibly any more room on your plate. Before you know if you are not living presently, you could end up with a full-on dinner-sized salad fully loaded to the max with every single salad ingredient you could find in your kitchen instead of a healthy little side salad for lunch like you originally had planned. You now have created this giant delicious salad in your mind, yet it might not be in your best interest to pig out on it. Ask yourself why you do this, and you might see that you are lost in the pleasure-seeking of the mind and not in the eating of the salad itself. You might end up throwing most of the salad away, but at the time, it sure was a wonderful concept as you kept adding more things of form to the creation of it until it couldn't possibly get any better.

This type of thing that constantly happens might not seem like much since the ego will tell you that it is just a salad, but the importance of remaining present in all areas of your life is extremely important. If you lose your self-awareness by living in the ego while making a simple salad, imagine the consequences of losing your ability to remain present while you are doing something really dangerous like riding a motorcycle on a busy freeway or driving a car while super tired. Your willingness to lose weight could easily take a back seat if you are laid up in the hospital because you were daydreaming or zoning out while doing something that puts your life at risk. Hopefully, you can see that even though presence is required to lose weight, it is also required while doing every single thing else in life no matter what form it takes. Living fully in the ego or autopilot works for most without question and will get everyone by, but it is also the reason for your unhappiness. It is the reason for reading this type of book. It is not a fulfilling life experience to get through twenty years of life and to look back and go where was I? Where did the time go? It is the reason we live a life of regret. It is the reason why we feel so trapped by our life circumstances, but it is also the reason why we just can't seem to find any self-discipline. We start any kind of plan to change something all gung-ho, but our effort fades pretty quickly. Old mental patterns set back in, and we end up feeling defeated over and over and over each time we try to change. We often think the method we are using is what is not working, but we never stop to realize that we cannot stay present with the changes we are trying to make that stops us each time.

The mind is extremely linear and always has one thought stacked on top of another thought until the result is a concept. There are just as many ways to lose weight as there are different ways to take different thoughts and arrange them to form new weight loss concepts. The ability to pick one that you are attracted to and to remain present enough to stick with every second of every day is the only way you will be able to lose all the weight you are seeking to lose. The reason you might have tried and failed in the past is simply because you might have remained present for a few days or a few weeks. However, the moment you lost that presence the weight immediately came back as your old pleasure-seeking eating habits returned.

The easiest way to remain present while attempting to lose weight is to flood your immediate awareness with all the weight loss tools that you can find. Keep a daily food log and write down every single thing you ate at what times and then get yourself a food scale and weigh everything out in portions. Start keeping track of the portions you eat to give you an idea of what is going on with your eating habits. Keep track of when you go to the gym or when you exercise. Maybe start small so that you are not going to the opposite extreme of your ego by demanding that you become a better person by losing weight.

Forcing change makes it twice as hard as accepting change. Instead, slowly return to the present moment with the form your weight loss routine is taking and learn to hold it firmly in your field of awareness. Losing weight is not making you a better person. You will still be the same person when you have lost weight because you are simply changing your daily habits! The feeling of being better is simply your willingness to accept the present moment because you have lost weight.

You could have experienced life the same way as a heavy person if you weren't so busy denying the present moment in its current form. The more you cling to the concept of weight loss, and the more you become aware of the selfishness of the ego as it relates to food, the more weight you will lose and the healthier you will become. Excellence or success is just a routine! There is nothing magical about losing weight, but our ego has a very long history of getting what it wants when it wants it and that is what is truly incredibly difficult to conquer. Learn to give up the extreme selfishness of the ego and no change cannot be easily and effortlessly accomplished.

Chapter 27

LIVE LIFE ABUNDANTLY

WE HAVE all heard of the concept of living an abundant life before, yet without the proper self-awareness or context, it simply gets put through the egoic filter of the mind and we automatically desire more things of form in abundance. The mind-dominated state of consciousness naturally assumes that abundance requires forms that we can experience with the five senses. We can be lost in a cycle of chasing down physical health, or financial wealth, or emotional happiness our entire life, and miss ever touching the present moment entirely if we are not careful. The ego instinctively desires to see more places, to taste better food and drink, to indulge more physically, to hear more pleasurable sounds, or to smell the sweetness of a particular fragrance.

When abundance arises in the mind, naturally we rush to gather and surround ourselves with more things or people or experiences. We get so lost in the ego experience once again as this new form of seeking ourselves in abundance arises that its only possible outcome is even further separation from our true selves or the present moment, and in doing so we miss the deepest connection or unity we can share with ourselves or all other conscious beings.

As another mind-dominated state of consciousness arises and this new form of self-seeking unfolds, we are so busy with the doing of the form, that we miss the true richness of non-doing or beingness that the present moment is so abundantly full of. After you have worked so hard collecting so many things of form, whether they are mental, physical, or emotional, what do you have left when it's all said and done? If your entire life is driven by this single concept of abundance, then you are probably pretty successful at it. You may very well end up being financially successful and having a ton of things of form to show for this self-seeking effort you have put forth. However, usually, in the end, most people who do this find themselves lost and alone because the depth of the mind never ends. It simply changes to the next form that you can lose yourself in and this can leave you burned out or tired of searching the world of form for the meaning behind your life.

The reason most people find themselves lost and alone is that this single mind-dominated concept revolves around selfishness. Even if you are surrounded by plenty of people in life, you are still stuck living in your mind. For instance, let's say you want to have an amazing relationship with your significant other, so you force them to do things that ultimately only make a great relationship in your mind such as going out all the time or taking trips, etc. It is so easy to get lost in doing all of these things with your partner that when the doing stops you feel lost in your relationship because there is no balance. You might believe you are making things better by forcing them to conform to your mental concepts about what makes a great relationship such as sitting on the couch with you every night to watch movies or spending "quality time" together, but really, it's quality time that your mind has deemed acceptable. You might be pushing the other person away because you have not once stopped to consider what their mind has deemed "quality time." They might feel forced to sit there. The problem with living in the mind while trying to attain abundance is it hardly leaves any room for actual reality to find its way into your conscious awareness. This is because the ego is always used to getting what it wants when it wants it. One of the biggest reasons life that is lived in the mind is called illusion is because what you are busy creating in your mind might be the polar opposite of what your partner is creating in theirs. This is why some people end up getting blindsided by a divorce. It can be because they are simply living a mind-created fairytale while the other person has been living a mind-created hell.

Balancing the awareness of what the egoic mind desires and the realization that you are not the mind is incredibly important if you want to keep your self-awareness while making your way through life and experiencing its abundance of forms. Instead of demanding that your partner sits on the couch with you every night, you need to have the realization that just because it is what your ego demands it doesn't necessarily make it right for your partner. Striking a balance between what you want and what your partner wants is the only way to maintain a healthy relationship. Sometimes that means not getting what you want, but not holding it against them either.

The most important thing about understanding egoic abundance is having the awareness that the mental seeking of it will not stop, it simply changes forms. Once you think you have something, the next thing pops into your mind and you are left seeking that out. Half of your life could be spent chasing down a career and once you believe in your mind that "you've made it." Only then does enough space in your consciousness present itself to release seeking yourself in that form for something new to arise such as starting a family and having children. The form it takes isn't important as it will always have a form of some kind. Hopefully, you don't spend your life chasing down mental concepts all the while missing out on true abundance that always exists in the present moment that is formless and can't be purchased with material or mental possessions. Having awareness of the present moment is what gives rise to the fullness of your being. It is where the true riches exist that nobody can ever take from you. No amount of chasing it down in the mind will ever get you there as it can't be thought up or experienced emotionally.

You can't build a house on a certain beautiful spot in the woods somewhere and call it the present moment because nothing of form can recreate it. Mental abundance can only be found by needing a "this" to cause a "that," experience. The abundance of the present moment stems from not needing anything of form to produce happiness. The awareness that you never needed anything of form to exist is what opens the door to touching this awareness.

At some point, there will always be an end to the mental abundance that is created. What happens when you get there? When you have all the money in the world and all the fame your ego craves, or the greatest relationship on earth, the mind will not stop, so what's next? What happens when the illusion is seen through and all of the things you believed made you live a life of abundance come crashing down? What happens when the house you built on that beautiful spot of land in the woods burns down? What happens when the career you've worked so hard for suddenly ends? What happens when the family or children you have made to be the source of your abundance suddenly dies? If any of these things completely rob you of all of the abundance that you had, then use that awareness as a pointer that you were stuck in a mind-dominated state of consciousness at the time. Just keep reminding yourself that true abundance does not depend on anything of form! Find out who you are with nothing or nobody and hopefully, someday you will truly touch the present moment and experience the abundance that is life itself!

Chapter 28

ADDICTION

ADDICTION IS an extreme attachment to pleasure seeking using a form that ultimately has the potential to ruin your life. The form it takes isn't important as it could be anything considered negative, but realizing how extremely selfish your ego has developed itself is the first step to shining a light on your addiction. The very first thing you have to do to kick any type of addiction is to bring awareness to the fact that you don't feel in control. Have you tried to stop something, but you just can't? Once you are no longer enjoying the form your ego has taken can you then attempt to experience the opposite.

Addictions can be great pointers to how unaware of the present moment you are. If something is happening that seems completely out of your control and you realize it is causing you suffering, then you have now taken the first step to release the ego experience enough by your desire to make a positive change in your life. This desire for change creates the smallest of openings that allow your consciousness to begin to shine through the destructive mental patterns that have you feeling so lost and out of control.

If you have an overeating problem, bring awareness to every single time you eat. If you have a drinking problem, focus on being present enough to consciously choose to drink every single time you consume your beverage of choice, it could even be a soda addiction. If you define yourself as a person with a great taste for fashion, then you automatically need to keep up with the ever-changing mental movements of designers and you could easily find yourself with an overspending problem that causes you suffering. People think of addictions as drug or alcohol related, but it can take on any form.

No matter what you deal with that you seem to be unable to control, the first step is to be present enough to catch yourself doing it before you do the thing that causes you suffering which you normally do without giving any thought to it. If you only have awareness of the ego, then you will completely disregard the thing you do the most. The drinking will just happen naturally as if it was just the usual thing to do when given the chance just as your lungs taking its next breath will happen without you choosing to do it every single breath. If you bring awareness to the drinking itself as a form, you will see how often you drink. If you do not pay close attention to the present moment, then how can you ever stop drinking when it's so programmed as a natural daily occurrence? I don't know anybody who just grabs a bottle and drinks in silence. The form of drinking is usually interconnected with other things like hanging out with friends or some form of entertainment that accompanies the drinking. The ego seeks to add things to the current moment, so whatever form the addiction takes, you will see that the thing you are addicted to is being added to something else to make the present moment somehow better.

When your conscious awareness is completely in a mind-dominated state, the ego experience is like a train, just heading to the next stop with complete disregard for the beautiful scenery along the way! It's kind of like saying the ego experience is like being born in the middle of the ocean and living your entire life there. You might have only ever known water, but the moment you see land for the first time is the moment self-awareness arises for the first time. Awareness of the present moment is the realization that there is something else existing at the same time other than only water. You may have spent your entire life only knowing one thing, but the moment you become aware of the opposite that exists at the same time is the moment you gain a greater context in which all things in the mind/body experience are held.

Chapter 29

THE EGO AND DISAPPOINTMENT

IN THE EGO EXPERIENCE, when disappointment arises, I notice it usually stems from a collapsing of mind-created illusions. One simple typical scenario would be to throw your significant other a nice dinner for their birthday. As you witness the mind arising in regard to this dinner, you will see all kinds of ideas and concepts flowing into your immediate mental awareness. You mentally sort through them one by one evaluating which one you feel will add the most to the future moment when you present them with a nice dinner and gift and in doing so will add a little worth to you in their eyes as well. You want to pick something that you feel will make them feel surprised at your thoughtfulness and you also want them to be extremely happy with your gift selection and effort.

The gift itself as a concept is just another egoic addition to the thought of oneself. As we all know there is no right or wrong in gift-giving, it's always the thought that counts. In this case, as you make your mental selection and settle on the perfect gift, even more illusions are created. Now that the mind has moved beyond the gift itself, you must create the perfect setting in which to present your gift. You can see the perfect place, and the perfect atmosphere to create to make it even more special. Let's say you envision a nice romantic candlelight dinner with a gift presentation at the end.

At this point, as you can see one form leads to another, which then leads to another and ultimately creates the illusion. As this concept of the perfect gift is unfolding in the mind, all of these new mental attachments are constantly being added to create one big overall illusion of perfection. You have mentally picked out the gift, you have mentally created the setting, and you have mentally picked out the perfect food for the dinner. Keep in mind all of this could have happened at the very first thought of making yourself responsible for their birthday happiness. None of this is a reality at this point, but instantly you have witnessed all these mental attachments arising and have then completely conceptualized the entire scenario.

Now let's say after all of this mental planning you attempt to make this perfect conceptualized birthday dinner and gift presentation a reality. Since most people are so busy these days, how do you go about getting the gift? Most people jump on the Internet and order the gift ahead of time and have it shipped directly to them. So now you have ordered the gift, you can check that off the list. Next, you have to round up the perfect candles and you need to completely clean your place and make sure everything is organized, you could have also put together the perfect music for the evening to set the mood, etc.

At this point, you could only be a day or two away and now you are getting excited. You could have held this perfect idea in your mind for a week or two now. You have gone through all the preparations to make this event perfect. Your spouse can probably see something weird is going on with you. They might even ask what you are up to because they notice a change in your attitude and behavior. You just smile and tell them you are just excited for their birthday, that's all. You are so wrapped up mentally in making this great big illusion a reality that you kind of forget about the normalcy of life and are more focused on this grand surprise you are attempting to create for them so you can experience some level of excitement and happiness over these thoughts.

So now let's say it's the day of their birthday. You go to work and your mind is flooded with all the last-minute preparations that you need to do. You don't want to be at work at all and now you feel hurried to get off and go shopping for the groceries and supplies needed for the big dinner. Once you get to the store and are going around picking out all the groceries, your mouth could be watering from how amazing you think the food is going to taste. You could have selected a dinner that is going to be a real treat.

Now the last thing you need could be a gift bag for the present. You can easily swing by another store and grab the perfect bag and some tissue paper. As you are on your way home, you have everything in your possession now to make this perfect plan a perfect reality. You excitedly hurry home, as you arrive you grab all of your bags of goodies and head inside your house only to find that your gift has been delivered and your significant other has already opened it even though it was sent to your name.

At this point, you stop dead in your tracks and drop all the bags as this huge wave of disappointment washes over you your mind-created illusions come crashing down and instantly you feel that everything is completely ruined. All of those weeks of planning this perfect evening and all of the mental and physical effort that was put forth have been ruined in an instant. As the happiness leaves and anger begins to fill the void, you can easily begin witnessing depressing thoughts arise as you feel as if something has been taken away from you.

The ego experience is selfish, so you completely fail to realize that this is their birthday and now you can begin yelling at them for opening the package. At this point, your ego can feel so completely wounded that you no longer wish to make them a nice dinner. Since your mind-created master plan didn't go exactly as it was supposed to, you probably don't want anything to do with the rest of the evening. You start to witness all of these negative mental movements arising and you can just start saying what instantly enters your mind.

The other person might not even understand what is going on at all and they can try to calm you down, but it probably won't make a single bit of difference. You are now fully engulfed in the mind-dominated egoic state of consciousness, and you might feel that you don't have any other choice other than to leave the house or continue to blame them for ruining everything.

You fail to see that the only thing that was ruined was your mind-created illusion. Nothing that you witnessed in your mind happened except your ego attempted to make the mental storyline a reality and failed. Instead of fully accepting the present moment in any form it takes. Instead, you have made a huge enemy out of the present moment, and in doing so, you could have ruined your significant other's birthday. Instead of making it a wonderful day for them no matter what, you selfishly went through all these different mental states of being because one thing didn't fall perfectly into place. You weren't present enough to just let go and let things be as they are, you instead fought and resisted the present moment once your ego didn't get its way.

This is just one simple everyday scenario; now imagine how many more different experiences you could have had like this when something didn't go your way. The form or example always changes. Today it was a birthday dinner, and tomorrow it could just be going out to dinner after work. Whenever you live in your mind, if those mental illusions are never fully manifested the way you desire, disappointment arises. When this disappointment is experienced, the ego usually will act out because the ego is selfish and always wants to get its way. The only way to end this egoic suffering is to fully accept the present moment no matter what form it takes or no matter what disappointment arises.

Chapter 30

THE EGO AND HARM

WHEN THE EGO attempts to harm another person, it does so because your ego has usually been hurt somehow or in some way. It goes back to the ego experience of having this need to witness opposing extremes. If you feel down, sometimes it makes you feel better to punish the person who you felt made you suffer. You immediately rush to experience the opposite of how horrible you feel. Harm is always justified by thinking, "Well, they have done something unpleasant to me, so I need to do something to them." It can be physically harmful, but most of the time it is just mental or emotional harm. During arguments, the egoic attachment starts small by yelling or calling names, as the attachment grows stronger so do the reactions. At first, you were yelling, now you could be throwing and breaking things.

You could seek to damage a material object that has a great mental attachment to the other person, and in doing so you are attempting to harm them. You think that somehow hurting them will make you feel better or more importantly that it proves you were right, and they were wrong for the way they treated you, so your actions are justified. The illusion of retaliation might seem like a real thing the moment it's happening, but as we all know eventually that high feeling of finally getting the better of someone who has caused you suffering is replaced by that low feeling of guilt and regret for stooping to that level.

People don't instinctively rush out to harm others; they usually do so in defense of their fragile egos. Something on some level of the ego-self has been diminished in some way, shape, or form. Once your ego has been diminished, the mental floodgates open and all of the other negative thought forms attached to the situation begin to arise giving the illusion that you need to react to the thoughts witnessed to keep your ego securely intact. It is because of how you think and feel in the present moment that everything in your mind is witnessed to be true, and even the most absurd possibilities that you would normally never consider when you are self-aware now seem to be a possible reality. The damaged ego could stem from a personal attack, or it could be much bigger such as an attack on the egoic structure of an entire nation. If you are not personally attacked, then perhaps your mental attachment to a particular group that you're affiliated with was attacked verbally or physically. Therefore, you feel a sense of duty to instinctively retaliate with the same force or even greater than what was done to you.

This is how feuds between people occur and it can grow exponentially depending on how many people are involved. You will see this egoic attachment in many groups across the world. Groups such as law enforcement, gangs, the military, or any group whose conceptualized form has some sort of violence attached to it whether the violence is deemed "required" to protect others or not. It all occurs because of the separation from the awareness of our consciousness. If we are not a consciousness-based society where the awareness that through consciousness, we are all unified to be the same thing taking on different forms. Then we are an egoic-based society which is a conceptualized individual that is completely different from every other being on earth, therefore it needs to fight for survival by being a part of something bigger for fear that it cannot survive alone.

In some form or another, the ego always has opposition. Opposing mental extremes allows any person the opportunity to attach oneself egoically to any group or situation. It is usually "me" or "us" against "them," or good vs. bad, right vs. wrong. For example, it could be law enforcement against criminals, this gang against a rival gang, or our military against their military. If one group member is attacked, the other members feel they have somehow been attacked as well. One big example here in the United States was 9/11. You had two opposing egoic mental points of view and when one of them was reacted upon, major suffering occurred. As you can see simply denying the present moment can do much harm, because the potential to go to a horrific extreme is always a possibility. In any event, in the ego experience, there is always a need to protect or defend this conceptualized self whether it is personally or globally. Suffering arises usually when there is anything to do with this conceptualized self which is why it is so important to know the opposite to exist between the two extremes.

The opposite extreme of the egoic state of mind is the present moment where everything exists perfectly as it is without needing to add or subtract anything. It is the deepest level of consciousness that is formless and has no body, nor does it witness the mind. It doesn't go to work to get a paycheck to survive in the world of form. It doesn't even need to eat food or breathe air to survive. It doesn't depend on a planet labeled Earth or even a solar system for that matter. It is the self of no self. It is the alpha and omega. It is the beginning of consciousness and the end of consciousness all at the same time. Ultimately, our consciousness just IS. It exists simultaneously in the world of form just as it is still formless. Form and formless are extremes, but consciousness is on the sideline watching the ego attempting to find itself in both extremes of the mind or body. It is only labeled consciousness as we know it, yet it is what makes it possible to witness that thought form called consciousness even arising. The ultimate self that has no self at all simply can never be harmed nor can it be killed any more than it had a birth or immanent death. If consciousness exists as something that never had a beginning, how can it ever truly have an end?

When you kill someone, ultimately you are only truly killing a mental concept you have of them. You can't destroy consciousness by destroying the human body. The physical body might no longer serve them a purpose and no longer be needed here in the world of form, but perhaps that body only served a purpose to teach you such things about your heavy attachment to the most horrific parts of your ego attachment. To harm or kill another being means to have never really lived at all, because you have yet to touch life deeply enough to understand it. Therefore, you have completely missed the point of life itself. The main point in life is to become aware of life itself, instead of being lost in the ego experience your entire life having only awareness of the mind/body, past/future. Additionally, the constant suffering that takes place in that experience and the separation from all others instead affords you to see the unity that is shared among all conscious beings.

The attempt to harm someone is one of the biggest illusions of the ego that allows for the majority of all human suffering to take place. The illusion that you can be harmed, and also the illusion that since you are harmed, you must in turn harm someone else. You see on the news every day where a "bad" guy kills a "good" guy. Then supposedly another "good" guy goes and kills the "bad" guy. The only thing separating the good guy that kills from the bad guy that kills is the egoic mental positioning. The real "good" guy is the guy who might witness the urge to attack or defend but can see both as just another egoic movement of the mind arising. If he can see it clearly, then no reaction to the witnessing of the passing thought form is required since he has an allowance for all things to arise at all times without the need to label or judge. If there is no action taken, then there can't possibly be any harm whether it is physical or by speech. If there is an action that requires a reaction, then that immediate reaction is your attachment to this fragile ego-self that can always be harmed therefore you feel it constantly needs verbal or physical defense, when ultimately you just need awareness of both extremes of the mind and a realization that you are neither so that you can remain centered in the present moment.

Chapter 31

EGO ON

IF YOU HAVE EVER PRACTICED Reiki, then saying Reiki on to activate Reiki is kind of like what happens when you completely lose all self-awareness, and the ego-self takes full control of the present moment. The only difference is practicing Reiki is a conscious choice that you can turn on and off at a time of your choosing. The ego-self that has the switch turned on without your approval is an instinctual reaction to what is happening to you physically, emotionally, or mentally without you choosing to lose yourself or lose control in the moment.

The ego-self that completely takes control when we are angry or somehow wounded is a certain aspect of the overall ego experience that leaves us completely helpless and at the mercy of our past conditioning. When you argue, it might be over something different all the time. But if you look closely, you will probably discover that it usually has the same beginning, the same middle, and the same ending.

The ego always goes back to what it knows and reacts the same way as it always has when the illusory self feels attacked in some way, shape, or form. The subject of the argument always changes with whatever you witness arising in the mind at the time. But does the act of arguing itself ever really change? You instantly react to something, you argue, then you either feel you've won the argument, or you simply refuse to argue anymore, and you give up and detach yourself from the act of arguing.

When the ego-self is fully active, the most selfish and defensive thoughts are witnessed arising and clung to as reality. You feel so put out by the thoughts you are unconsciously attaching yourself to that you instinctively lash out at those you perceive as wounding you. You want them to feel some sort of pain and suffering even if it's just a little bit verbally, as you too are feeling pain and suffering at the time. This aspect of the ego-self could activate over something that happened outwardly that you mentally have not made an allowance to arise, such as another person that you don't know calling your lover or your kids doing something that you never expected them to do. It could be a bit of road rage that sparks this arising of negativity, etc. It doesn't have to be anything big to activate this ego-self, it just has to be something that happens to you that makes you feel wronged or diminished somehow.

For some people who experience this activation of that aspect of their ego that requires a battle of some sort, it seems so real that sometimes it just can't be let go of without the proper defense or even counterattack. They continue to drag around with them a mental grudge for a certain amount of time. It could be an argument that happened between friends or even a couple, and this mental division in their relationship could carry on for days, weeks, or even months. In the case of a married couple, it could carry on for years until eventually you finally break up because you were not able to return to the present moment. This is how you get up to a divorce or go through with a divorce to return to the present moment and realize you were foolish and made a mistake and end up wanting them back. You will realize that the only thing that changes after a divorce is your willingness to let go of the past and return to the present moment!

Communication is the key to dealing with this particular aspect of the ego experience. It is a terrible feeling when it happens, but it isn't only a personal experience because it will happen to them as well. The only difference will be the form it takes. If you become aware of this experience and know when it triggers inside yourself first of all, then you need to share it with your partner. Help them become aware of what this is when it happens not only to you but to them as well. Then learn together to spot it as it is happening before it takes a nasty form and carries on as a "real thing" between you or if anything after it has happened. If you can put your finger on exactly what it is, then eventually you will no longer need to argue or fight again.

I think it is really helpful to understand that this experience is not just about you, as it happens to every person on earth before they become aware of it! The wounded ego of another will always attempt to make you feel like less of a person during an argument. Unfortunately for them, they don't realize when the wounded ego activates there is no real "you" to speak of at the wheel steering the form of an argument as it is happening. You can both attempt to lessen each other with words or concepts, but ultimately it will unfold as it always does with you both speaking exactly what is being witnessed arising in the negative mind at that moment.

The kinder and gentler non-attached you that is normally able to choose your words with love and affection when you are more present is covered up by the wounded and defensive heavily attached ego-self that has a big storyline of past events dragging along behind it. These past events are how your ego seeks to attack their ego by attempting to prove you are somehow lesser based on past actions and words. You can only wound them mentally, but only if they believe in this ego-self that you are attempting to attack. These pointless egoic attacks might work on a person who only has awareness of an ego-self, but ultimately, it's not even possible to attack a fully self-aware person, as there is no self to speak of.

As always, awareness is the key, if you are unaware then your ego-self is the puppet master pulling on the strings of the present moment. In the end, you both either have awareness and can let go of the mind and be free to experience the present moment together, or you can carry on the rest of your life believing everything that you witness in the mind is absolute reality. Arguments and unawareness go hand in hand, for without one, you can't have the other. The trick to bringing awareness to the present moment is to simply STOP right as your wounded ego-self becomes active and starts to defend itself. Then ask yourself what happens if you do nothing or say nothing. Subsequently, you will see that this aspect of your ego can't possibly carry on if you willingly deny the battle before it ever has a chance to continue to arise and gets completely out of your control.

Chapter 32

CULTURE AND EGO

IN THE EGO EXPERIENCE, the depth that a particular culture or society takes is based on a running total of all experiences of a particular group of people, who have at some point separated themselves from others to form their own conceptualized beliefs. Years upon years of building on a single belief or a single thought possibly leads an entire civilization through an endless cycle of suffering. Even if the initial belief was considered good and just, the ways that mind-dominated people twist the initial belief to suit their own needs can cause tremendous suffering. The only way to break the cycle of suffering is by allowing the original belief to progress and evolve to meet current needs and conditions. Ways of the old don't always have our best interests in mind if they are not given the ability to balance themselves with what was working in the past and what is working in the present. The question should arise, "Who are we as a people now?" Not to be stuck in the thought, "This is who we have always been, so we must continue for fear that we will lose ourselves or our culture."

The hardest thing for a society to do is change. The easiest thing for a society to do is to continue doing the same things while expecting different results. True change comes only when fear of loss is relinquished. If the thought of change arises, then fear will naturally arise also. Fear that if we do not continue doing what we have always done, then we will be lost, and we won't be able to define ourselves.

The mind needs a history for the egoic structure to remain intact. If a person woke up from a coma with complete amnesia, how would they know who or what to be? Without a history, then how is the mind to know what it is supposed to do or think right now in this moment? Doesn't fear arise when the illusion of the mental security we have constructed over the years comes crumbling down? Can you imagine if an entire nation went through cultural amnesia? What would be left? What would they do? You will probably see an answer to this as a big shift is happening in the Middle East where tyranny is no longer an illusion the people are willing to maintain. Once the power or control that was placed on people is removed, you will see a rebirth of freedom. Many things that were culturally unacceptable before will now be given a chance to emerge.

What is normally the first thing you see in movies when someone has amnesia? They ask the doctors, "Who am I," or "Where am I?" It is a good pointer to the fact that the mind still requires that definition of self and has an overwhelming need to piece together everything it is reacting to forming some type of identity with its current surroundings. When people are no longer forced to be a certain thing, they will instinctively start looking for answers to new questions that are arising. If one form of ego is all you have known and then all of a sudden you are set free, what is the first thing you would do? Probably the opposite of what you have been forced to do, forced to think, and forced to believe. When looking at an entire culture or society from your egoic point of view, try to see them with compassion as you will find that many people had to do horrible things to survive. If you as an individual were given a choice to conform to the beliefs of someone in power or die, what would you choose? Even if you were given that kind of a choice in your past and you chose survival, is it okay? It is the instinct of the ego. The best thing about the present moment is when you are no longer willing to drag your past with you, you will find freedom no matter what you had to do to survive. What would your life be like if you could wash away all of the selfish misdeeds of the fearful ego?

That question can be answered in your lifetime once you gain true awareness of the present moment where the culmination of your ego is not completely dominating your awareness. The present moment is the only opportunity we have available to us that needs no egoic definition. It is completely free from the suffering of the past or the possible suffering from thoughts of the future. Luckily, the present moment isn't as extreme as requiring you to lose all of your memories to experience it. You will still have the awareness of your ego, yet you will no longer solely depend on it to exist. The mental attachment to living in the past will no longer dominate your existence the more you learn to remain fully present. Remaining fully present gives you the ability to completely wipe your slate clean and for the first time gives you a truly fresh start no matter what you did in your past even if others aren't so quick to forgive you.

Chapter 33

EMOTIONS AND FEELINGS

IN THE EGO EXPERIENCE, emotions and feelings make up a substantial part of the human experience itself. It is through these emotions and feelings that people feel they touch life deeply or the very things that make them feel human. It is through the witnessing of these arising emotions and feelings that many of our most important life choices are based. When a thought arises and is witnessed and an emotion that accompanies that thought also arises and they are added together, they form a mind-dominated reality. One great pointer to this state of awareness is when you are only able to see one possible solution to a situation and an immediate reaction is experienced. That is ego. One example you have seen time and time again is when a person commits a severe crime. If the present moment gets away

from them to the point that they feel they just can't live with the consequences; they can commit suicide.

That one extreme of the mind-dominated state of consciousness that has arisen and is labeled me is what leaves you completely stuck in the ego experience. You might witness negative thoughts and emotions arising and act out instinctively in a violent uncontrollable way. You might experience the opposite and witness very loving and compassionate thoughts and emotions arising and end up doing something you regret later when they pass like cheating on someone. No matter which extreme is experienced, regret usually is a tell-tale sign that the ego is in full control, and it's only realized once the illusion is seen through and self-awareness returns. When you find yourself asking, "What was I thinking?" you pretty much need to realize you were not thinking anything at the time, as you were not deeply grounded in the present moment. You instead, were simply *reacting* to witnessed thoughts and emotions arising in that moment. It is only when the reaction stops and you can disconnect from the situation that are you able to gain perspective on what happened. You could either have ended up in jail or love depending on the situation. Both of these can leave you regretting the unawareness that was experienced at the time.

Ultimately, emotions and feelings are just another aspect of the mind/body experience that is witnessed and the only true meaning behind them is the meaning you come up with in your mind. I have seen great suffering with people who only associate themselves with the emotional aspect of the ego. They experience life in such a way that non-stop emotions are witnessed arising and they do not possess the self-awareness that they cannot cling heavily to them. Each emotion to them is experienced as absolute reality and you can't convince them otherwise. It is only when they have hit their emotional rock bottom and are willing to give up their attachments to emotions completely that they can return to the present moment to find the end of their suffering.

Feelings work the same way, have you ever had a thought that just made you feel sick to your stomach? Have you ever wondered if you never had that thought in the first place if you would still feel sick? Your ego fights for survival and this survival instinct is based on the denial of unpleasant thoughts and feelings and seeks survival by immediately replacing them with pleasurable thoughts and feelings. Have you ever felt down and immediately wanted to go do something that you knew would make you feel better? Most women that I know instinctively run out and have a girl's day shopping. They want to replace the negative thoughts and feelings with more desirable thoughts and feelings. The ego attempts to take the attention off what is being witnessed arising for fear that it is somehow diminishing them, and it rushes to pleasure seek in some other form. Somehow, that is an addition to your ego-self. It's kind of like the ego robs Peter to pay Paul. It reacts in such a way that it covers up a previous problem with a new one. Only, the new solution is absolutely no different from the old one; it has just taken a different form and is labeled acceptable.

You can now witness new feelings arising based on pleasurable thoughts, but it's the same thing. You still have an arising of feelings and thoughts, but now the concept of good is placed on them. There is still an egoic reaction that is taking place based on what you're witnessing in the present moment. Your day has not changed for the better, because you are still lost attempting to find yourself in those thoughts and feelings. You can run away from bad ones all day long, but until you have the proper understanding of what is going on, your life will be a roller coaster ride of suffering. You will always have your ups and downs and can always label them good or bad depending on how you want to feel, but ultimately, you need to know they are all just egoic attachments to a self that doesn't even exist. The illusion is so strong that we all do it, and it's the only thing that we have ever known how to do our entire lives. Nobody has ever once told us that we were able to just accept everything that arises in the present moment without rushing to label it good or bad. Nobody ever said that by fully accepting all things of form, as they are that all of our suffering will end. It's the denial of the arising of forms that gives birth to suffering. We each can witness without losing our self-awareness in that witnessing. We can unconditionally accept everything that we think, feel, and experience without allowing it to lift us or bring us down in some way, shape, or form.

Emotions and feelings can be a wonderful part of the mind/body experience as long as you don't completely lose yourself in them. They arise out of nothingness and then are witnessed, and if accepted just as they are without adding anything egoically to it, they will gently subside back into the nothingness of the present moment. It is the clinging to them as they arise that gives them the ability to seem real as if it was actually how you felt and dictates how you need to react. The clinging is what gives the feelings and emotions its life span. The length of the clinging dictates the length of the witnessing of the emotions and feelings themselves. If you cling heavily to a loving emotion, it can be with you for years until one day it just subsides, and you can instinctively react and convince yourself that your marriage is over. If you cling heavily to a negative emotion, such as anger, it can be with you for years until one day it just subsides, and you are no longer willing to call a certain person your enemy. Just be mindful of both extremes of emotions. Feelings arise and subside constantly, but if you cling to neither and accept both extremes just as they are without the desire to change either, then freedom from suffering will occur and you will find your salvation right now in the present moment.

Chapter 34

DON'T BLAME OTHERS

ONE OF THE biggest survival mechanisms of the ego is to blame others for your own problems for your ego to maintain its structural integrity. Let's say you can't get along with someone. Is that their fault that you are denying the present moment in whatever form it has taken with them? Is it their fault that you witness so many negative thoughts and emotions that your ego takes it all out on them for the sake of their survival? If you weren't able to blame others for your out-of-control thoughts, feelings, and emotions, your ego would crumble under its weight, and you would feel completely lost and confused. It's part of the ego's defenses to drag along the history of another person and to use it as ammunition to attempt to wound their ego to maintain your own. When you deny the present moment, a big pointer to this fact is when you cannot stop yourself from pointing out all of their faults constantly. You can accept them for all of the things they are, but you are not able to accept them for all the things they are not. That type of conditional acceptance is hugely ego-driven and as you can see does not lead to unconditional love for others.

When you are arguing with someone, your ego seeks out the comfort and support of others during these times when it's fragile. You have probably seen it a hundred times. After a huge argument, you immediately scramble around, calling people up and trying to explain how you are right and the other person is wrong. Your ego is seeking survival by needing the approval of others when this happens. It's not a right or wrong situation. It is an egoic reaction vs. a non-egoic reaction that either leads to suffering when you react or peace when you do not react. If you were to witness all of the mental and emotional forms arising during the argument, but did nothing to act on them, they would pass, and the peace would return. If you immediately, without thought, just said and felt the things you were witnessing, then suffering arises for both people. The need to blame others is an attempt to salvage some sense of self that needs to be right in every situation. Ask yourself. What is an apology? Is it some magical word that fixes everything? Is it instead a willingness to let go of the past and return to the present moment, which is the only place where peace is truly found? The only way you can ever truly win in any situation that causes suffering is if you deny the battle before it ever gets started. Ultimately there is absolutely no need to blame others for anything. Instead, you need to learn to accept the present moment in any form it takes, and that only comes from true self-awareness. The ego awareness will always leave you playing the blame game!

Chapter 35

EGOIC ESCAPISM

Have you ever felt like not doing anything makes you go stir-crazy? Have you ever felt like you are not making any progress in life if you are not actively moving forward toward a particular goal or some form of happiness? Have you ever been injured and just been forced to sit still for an uncomfortably long amount of time? Have you ever had a drinking or drug problem and ran out of them and couldn't get more? How deeply connected to the "doing-ness" of something, like a career or a particular hobby, are you? How often does the form of what you do or feel you need to do to survive dominate your life? All of those thought forms that I have stated come complete with their feelings and emotions. If we all remember how we felt when one of them arose in our life, then we can all remember exactly how the pull of the ego feels. It is things of this nature that are another great pointer to how deeply rooted in the ego experience each one of us is, and we don't know it until we aren't able to continue doing something we have always done or want to do and that is when suffering arises.

When you are fully immersed in the ego experience, there is no awareness of it. Yet when you are forced out of the flow of the ego experience and back into the present moment where nothing is added, for some, it can seem like the worst thing in the world. When you are fully dominated by the ego experience, the form that your habits take can feel like your very salvation. It can feel as if the thing you do or want to do the most is your therapy. It can also be experienced as an escape or this place you go to find peace where you don't witness the suffering of the mind arising and subsiding any longer. For most of us, we go to work and try to get it out of the way for the day so we can come home and enter that state of release. In other words, doing something we want instead of doing something we feel forced to do. For some of us, we only do the things we feel forced to do and nothing more during the week, feeling kind of worn out and miserable along the way, to escape and do what we want on the weekends seeking freedom from the same old weekday form that has been beating us into submission our entire adult lives.

Experiencing life this way is another great pointer to the opposing extremes of the mind-dominated state of consciousness. We fail to see that both extremes are the same thing taking on different forms because we are busy feeling lost or even angry in the part of the form that is labeled bad or unpleasant, and busy finding ourselves feeling relieved in the part of the form that is labeled good or pleasant. We never realize that there is always something undesirable that is eventually replaced with something more desirable because no thought is given to the egoic extremes. This yin/yang effect is a great pointer to the egoic state of awareness. Some people will go into the yin aspect of life to find themselves and call this the right way to live, while others attempt to find themselves in the yang aspect and call that the right way. This separation that occurs by the need to define yourself somehow is the ego experience, yet until you understand that the differences of the yin/yang are only an illusion and are only witnessed in the mind-dominated state of consciousness. You will only know the suffering of the ego. It is only when you can accept both as the same thing taking on different forms that you are finally able to see the unity that all of mankind shares through consciousness. When the present moment is truly witnessed, the end of all human suffering will be found, for the separation that exists between all others only does so in the mind.

We also fail to realize that one form is no different from another because in the mind they are considered complete opposites due to conceptualized labels. It can be absolutely anything of form that we can attempt to find ourselves in, from the doing-ness of a career to projects around the house, from playing video games to doing your favorite hobby. Once a major thought form is experienced, it begins to dominate your awareness; therefore, it constantly arises. Sooner or later, if no conscious awareness is given to it, then it simply becomes your life or the way you are. It's only when you are forced out of that flow of living everyday life as you have that self-awareness emerges enough for you to look around and go, "Hmm? How did I get here?" For example, think of someone who just got clean in rehab for the first time in years and self-awareness returned enough to realize how lost in the ego experience or the forms of drinking or drugs they were.

Usually, the question that also arises is more importantly, "What's next?" The ego experience stops for nobody typically and there always is a need for a continuation of some sort to how you have always lived life. You hear stories every day of how someone you know was doing so good in rehab, then once they got out, they just went back to life as they knew it before they entered rehab. This is because their egoic definition of themselves never changed. It only subsided while in rehab which was uncomfortable and caused them suffering because of how great the pull of the ego can be. They never let go of the storyline which is why they constantly battle it after rehab. I think a common misunderstanding when dealing with addiction is the unawareness of the egoic attachment a person has to the form that they find themselves in. It's not the particular circumstance such as drinking, drugs, or even sex addiction, that has the power over them, it's their inability to deny the desires of their egoic attachments that is the true addiction. The form of the particular addiction can be different for everybody, but the root cause of the problem is always the same. Once released from their program, the pull of the ego will inevitably arise once again, and they will be left alone to choose for themselves whether to react and go back deeper into the form. Or they may not react and let it subside by doing nothing to act on the thoughts and feelings witnessed.

The selfish ego always desires to add some sort of pleasure seeking to the nothingness of the present "sober" moment, which is why non-reaction becomes such a tough thing to conquer. We all know that the concept of sober means nothing is added, and the ego always seeks to add something to the present moment over accepting nothingness. Just as a sober person adds something like a card game to the present moment, which barely covers up the nothingness, a person fighting addiction wants to add something extreme that fully covers up the nothingness of the present moment. They want to completely indulge in the mind/body experience. The only way a person truly leaves rehab and stays clean for the rest of their life is if they are willing to seek their ego-self in the soberness of the present moment or to leave behind the doing-ness or constant pull to pleasure seek and are willing to fully accept that being alive or able to witness the present moment by itself is a whole lot better than being completely out of control and at the mercy of a particular thought form or even eventually dead because they couldn't let go long enough to find peace in the present moment.

The problem is most people don't want to escape that flow of "doing-ness." They would rather be stuck in it as much as possible because that is therapeutic to them. The sameness of their daily routine is what the ego seeks because that is pleasurable and comforting to their mind as it is their safe place. They do not know the aspect of the self that has no self and needs nothing of form to exist. They only know the constant pull towards doing more, having more, needing more, and being more. They could be making the present moment better somehow by adding something to it. Even the thought that after they die, they may want to leave a big legacy behind, so they continue pushing forward as hard as possible for as long as possible. That push forward is what leaves people locked in the ego experience, and it is what gives them that sense of needing to accomplish something huge to feel satisfied with themselves or to prove that they have lived a life worth living, or to have done better than all of their friends. The opposite is a person who stops caring what people think about them and stops caring about what they think of themselves and just accepts staying lost in whatever form dominates their life out of pure self-ishness.

For most, they seek themselves in something they deem good and are comforted by pushing hard to be growth-oriented. When they are fully in the mix of it all and just doing their thing and the totality of their entire attention is focused on it, they can enter a Zen-like state, where they feel like they have escaped the clutches of the world. That aspect that can be experienced by losing yourself deeply in the world of form is seductive and is chased day after day. Think of a car salesman who is always chasing down a sale. Once he gets it, it's like bliss. Picture an athlete who is always chasing down a win, and once they get it and the crowd goes wild, it is pure bliss.

Ultimately, it's a great experience as it's happening, but just like all things in life, it doesn't last. Therefore, it leaves you chasing it down constantly and is responsible for causing suffering to you and those around you, as you are not present for them or even yourself.

The easiest way to spot an illusion is to ask yourself if the form you are seeking is eternal. The reality is anything that has a form is not eternal or will ever be eternal no matter how long it is experienced. Even if you are born into money and it lasts your entire life, the moment you die that form subsides for you and arises for another, so it was never an eternal form you experienced. It was only an illusion. The easiest way to see this is to look at any old Egyptian tomb that was stuffed with treasure for the king in his afterlife. Was the king able to use his treasure after he died, or did it just sit there waiting for some archeologist to discover it and put it on display in a museum?

Selling a car isn't eternal. It's just a thought form, just as winning a sporting event isn't eternal it also arises and subsides. You are only as good as the form you seek as long as you work at keeping the illusion alive. If you stop selling the most cars, then you are no longer the best at what you do, the same is true if you stop winning ball games. When the awareness of this begins to grow, then your egoic attachment diminishes, which now allows for some space to return to the present moment. You can still have the same experiences without giving them extra meaning or importance in your mind.

You can now stop chasing down those car sales all day every day as they will always be there, and more space will become available when the narrow-minded focus of the ego subsides. When freedom arises, as the clinging to the ego is released, you will find that you can make time for others, like your spouse or children, and still maintain outward success. You can even be a professional athlete and learn to enjoy life as it's happening instead of only when you are winning. The egoic escapism is strong, but detachment from these outward mind-dominated states of consciousness is the only way you can experience presence. You can find true peace and happiness right now even as you are reading this. It doesn't depend on a "this" causing a "that." The car sale won't produce true happiness, it only produces more illusions that the ego finds itself in.

Hopefully, you can see that letting life pass you by and not being present for those who love you the most is the biggest failure in life. To have lived a full and present life and to have found the end to your suffering all the while having accomplished all the other things you have wanted to regardless of financial success in the process is a great achievement indeed!

Chapter 36

YOU DID THIS TO YOURSELF

Have you ever heard anybody explain that you're in a certain negative position in life by looking at you with an uncompassionate heart and saying something like, "You did this to yourself!" It usually arises in the ego experience when something undesirable has happened, or you have hit this point in your life where you just end up in a place that is nowhere near what you wanted or ever expected to be. At the point when you are feeling down and at your worst, or even just lost and confused, someone else on their high horse gives you their two cents worth by explaining how you knew the rules of life but broke them.

Almost as if they are saying you wanted to experience the very thing that is causing you the most suffering in your life and were completely aware of it as it was happening the entire time. It could be anything from gaining a bunch of weight over several years or even getting divorced to somehow ending up in jail. It can be anything where others can look at you and sit back in the comfort of their ego, and without any compassion for your situation, they lay blame on you for not being fully and completely in total control of the outcome of your life.

It's another great pointer to the fact that when you are not fully present in the moment, you are lost in the ego experience just doing what you have always done without giving any thought to consequences that eventually accumulate over the years (i.e., overeating, smoking cigarettes, heavy drinking, selling drugs, etc.). Eventually, five years of big meals and no exercise catches up, and you realize for the first time just how overweight you are. Eventually, after forty years of smoking cigarettes, the doctor tells you that you now have lung cancer. Eventually, so many years of heavy drinking leave you flat broke, divorced, and possibly suicidal for losing everything. Eventually, after selling drugs for however long the police raid your house and you go to jail.

All of these examples are the same thing taking on different forms. They all point to a deep level of unawareness of the present moment, and it points to the flow of the ego experience. It consumes you with things you have always done and how you never really gave any thought to it as it was happening. If someone showed you a picture of how you would look in five years and told you how you would eventually feel about being overweight, would you have ever started to overeat? If someone told you that you would absolutely without a doubt die from lung cancer, would you ever have picked up the first cigarette? If you ever imagined that your quality of life would consist of hangovers and drinking binges that end up costing you your career, marriage, or even your life, would you have ever wanted to take your first drink? If someone told you that by selling drugs to only your friends you would eventually end up in jail for several years, would you ever have wanted to let greed dominate your life to the point of going to prison?

These are all very simple questions posed by the mind-dominated state of consciousness, but none of them have a simple answer since society is built on conceptualized past/present/future experiences of the mind. So, you have no way to explain how silly the concept is that you were consciously choosing every time that you did something that would ultimately cause you suffering when you were not. We all know that is never true. Nobody wants to suffer. The ego attempts to cover up suffering by creating mind-dominated illusions such as thought forms that supposedly create pleasurable experiences like eating good food, sharing a cigarette and drink with a friend, or even selling someone marijuana. The mind is also based on cause and effect, it will lead you to believe that because this happened you must have fully and willingly accepted the consequences of past actions as if you were self-aware.

If a habit was created and the awareness that ultimately everything that exists in the mind has an opposite is not known, then it should be easy to see how every person can lose themselves in the form their ego is taking at the time, and it then just becomes "life" and no longer a choice that is made every single second of every single day. The mind creates a reality whereafter it's already too late to do anything about. It believes that you had a choice knowing full well the consequences of your actions. The mind-dominated state unfortunately only gives you the awareness of the ego-experience and doesn't allow you access to the freedom of the present moment where unconditional love and acceptance are found and also life itself or the very ability to choose what to experience next instead of being controlled by past mental attachments. So, the next time a person looks at the form your egoic experience has taken, you can easily see now how it gives rise to their uncompassionate point of view, where in their mind they are living a life that is right, and you have lived a life that is wrong, and therefore, "You did this to yourself!"

The reality is that you didn't do anything to yourself other than live a life of unawareness of the present moment, and full awareness of an egoic sense of self that was always pleasure-seeking in any form that had arisen and not realizing what it was doing as it was happening. It is only when you stop and disconnect from the egoic experience that you see that you are practically a zombie, experiencing all of life's ups and downs and reacting to each of them instinctively to remain in a mind-created illusion of non-suffering. Little did you know that all of your attempts to live a life of non-suffering are actually what can truly create a life of suffering for you down the road. If you do not learn how to touch the present moment deeply enough to stop the flow of the ego experience and to disconnect from the mind/body association being the only thing you have ever known. All of the sufferings of the world are created by the ego's attempt to prove that good vs. bad and right vs. wrong exist so that you can be judged accordingly by whoever's mind-dominated state is being witnessed at the time in their attempt to judge you based on their past conditioning that they consider better or right.

Ultimately, you will see that there never was any true past conditioning, there was only the present moment in whatever form it took and now is being challenged by the mind to seek another egoic victory that says my life is right and unfortunately for you, your life was wrong because "You did this to yourself!"

Chapter 37

MIND VS. SELF-AWARENESS

IN THE MIND-DOMINATED state of consciousness, the awareness of the mind/body experience is the only thing that is witnessed; therefore, it is the only thing that is reacted to as if everything you can think or even conceive of is absolutely real. When you see only one way out of any given situation or scenario, it is a great pointer to the fact that you are fully stuck in the mind-dominated state of consciousness. It can include witnessing thought forms that take your awareness ever deeper into a reality that doesn't exist. For example, have you ever been cheated on, or even thought it could be a possibility? When the awareness of an ego-self that has been wronged by someone you loved, it can leave you locked in a state of being that is so horrible that there seems like no escape from it. That is unless you completely attempt to run away from the thoughts or try to get away from the other person by leaving them or erasing any mental attachment to them, such as hiding or destroying pictures of them or anything that reminds you of them. The moment it enters your mind that they cheated until the time after you take all of these steps to accuse them or divorce them or break up with them, all the way eventually until enough time has passed that it finally subsides, and you are finally able to get some mental peace, the total of that entire experience is the mind- dominated state of consciousness. There is no peace found in it, there is only doing-ness to alleviate suffering based on current mental mind movements.

Let's say you never even caught them, or they never felt guilty and admitted it if they did. Let's say you just suspect that they are cheating, and everything from that point on becomes proof that they are. When these types of thought forms are witnessed, there seems no end to them. Every little word or connection between them and another person is now given an entirely different meaning than before you ever suspected them of cheating and now more suffering arises. The mind has infinite possibilities to choose from, so there is never a shortage of opportunities to further your suffering on this matter. You could be paying attention to their habits and giving each one a negative meaning such as why did they shower after they came home late, when normally they might not? Why did it take them an extra hour or two to get from point A to point B? Who is it they are constantly text messaging? Why is it that every time I leave them alone, I feel they are taking that opportunity to cheat? Why is it that when I think about them cheating on me my stomach hurts? Where did the love go? Why do they keep telling me I'm crazy and have nothing to worry about when this feels so terrible and real? That self-suffering is one way to experience it. The other is to attempt to keep your ego-self fully intact and to rush out and surround yourself with other people to make your partner jealous. You can even find yourself cheating on them by doing this very thing because the ego is all about pleasure-seeking. When you are witnessing a very unpleasurable thought, such as being cheated on, you can ultimately do the thing you despise just to cover up your fears. You may not even realize it is happening until it is too late.

As you can see, the awareness of these thought forms has different extremes, but it also has no end. This tiny list just scratches the surface of the suffering that is experienced when you are fully in a negative mind-dominated state of consciousness. Cheating is just one single example of a thought form where if given enough attention it can take you down a terrible road of suffering that can lead to the end of your relationship when the reality of it is they might not have cheated at all. However, because you have made a mental enemy out of the present moment, you created a reality in your mind that leads you to fully believe they did. This experience can go on for days, months, or years based on one arising thought form that is clung to and is never allowed to subside possibly until it is too late, and your relationship ends because of it. Everything that is witnessed in the mind arises and is reacted based on the concept of your fragile ego-self that can feel hurt or wounded by one single negative thought. It can cause you a tremendous amount of mental and physical suffering if you do not learn how to become self-aware when it is happening. It is the awareness that it is happening while it is happening that means you become self-aware. The realization that it happened after it is too late doesn't do you any good other than to be another pointer to how insane the ego experience can be if left to run its course without your ability to choose what you want to experience at the moment.

Self-awareness is that tremendous space that exists in the present moment where no reaction to such thoughts or even the reality of someone cheating on you is experienced. It is that peaceful place that exists that holds your salvation when you lose your connection with the present moment enough to experience such suffering of the mind/body experience. It can only be accessed by the willingness to let go of all things of form by letting the negative thoughts subside, and letting the negative feelings and emotions that accompany those thoughts also subside. Self-awareness is that voice of reason that pops up and says, "Is this necessary?" It is that ability to stop the current course of actions based on negative thoughts; it is the realization that you are just playing the role based on a wounded ego-self that is fighting for survival by pushing away the other person in hopes of ending the suffering. The problem is no matter how far you attempt to distance yourself from these mental/emotional forms, they are illusions that are given form. These illusions can arise and subside at any given time based on the interconnectedness of everything else you are experiencing in the world of form at the time.

Let's say you divorced your partner based on a thought form of them cheating, and no matter how much they denied it and told you they loved you; it just wasn't possible to believe them based on your thoughts. So, after you move out and move on with your life believing they are practically one of the worst and most disgusting people you have ever met, somewhere down the road you find an old picture of you guys lying around. Since we live in a world of opposites, either one of two things happens. First, you can see the picture and all of the past conditioning arises and you are instantly witnessing the sick stomach and negative thoughts about how they did you so wrong and how you are so much better than them because you never would have cheated. Or the opposite, where you see their picture and feel some sort of remorse for not being able to remain present for them, witnessing the realization that they never might have done anything wrong and you were just so out of control at the time that you caused the entire relationship to come crashing down for no reason at all. The best you can hope for in any relationship is that you are fully present and self-aware and able to make decisions based on that awareness; otherwise, all of your decisions are based on the ego, and that will usually leave you all alone in the end. As you can see, no matter what arises at the time the picture is found, something will inevitably arise. This is the nature of the mind/body experience. There always has to be something arising and subsiding or we wouldn't have a need to witness the world of form.

Self-awareness is the only thing we need to find in this life and the only thing that I know of that can end all human suffering. You can live a life full of drama and unsubstantiated mental realities that have past or future egoic movements to them, or you can live a life centered in the present moment where self-awareness dominates the mind/body experience. No matter what is witnessed arising and subsiding there will always be the peacefulness of the formlessness of consciousness before anything in the world of form ever has a chance to be clung to and called real. Ultimately, suffering only exists in the mind and if we only know the mind-dominated state of consciousness, we only truly know suffering in any form it takes!

Chapter 38

DEFINITION REQUIRED TO ENTER

THE BASIS for all egoic reactions to arise is that the ego requires a complete definition of itself to maintain the illusion that it is a real thing. Without a perfectly defined self that is fully accepted as real, how would each of us know how to react or even what to react and not react to in our daily lives? How would we know what we like and do not like? How are we able to react to something we label good if we don't first instinctively label the opposite bad? The only thing required to enter the ego experience is the need to define everything around you at all times and to use that definition of life and everything included in it to allow your ego the ability to react accordingly. The ego experiences these reactions based on past conditioning. If we do not let go of this need to react to life, then we will never experience the ability to end all of the suffering that is experienced in this world based on the individualized ego being the center of the known universe.

First off, the need to define life is to limit life. There is no possible way you can experience a full amazing life if you are knowingly or unknowingly finding yourself existing in the definition of life that is created in your mind. There is no great big, amazing life that is being experienced. There is only a tiny little narrow-minded ego-self that has attempted to define itself either as happy or as sad, but it is boxed in on all sides and surrounded by egoic barriers. The barriers could be from the viewpoint of a happy life, and your life will only remain happy as all of the things that surround you are kept in place at all times. If one thing is taken away like the person you love the most, then your definition switches from happy to sad instantly.

This is how you know these egoic definitions are illusions because they are not eternal and they only last as long as something of form is kept securely fastened in your immediate awareness. Once the mental illusion of good is released based on a reaction to the death of a loved one, it is immediately replaced with a new attachment to sadness. These shifting mental movements are the bread and butter of the ego experience. Without them, how could you possibly gain or lose any ground in life in the ego's attempt to be better than others? It is this attempt to have more than others to keep up the illusion of happiness that allows for these extremes to be experienced.

If you were no longer ego-oriented and no longer in competition with the rest of the world, there would only be peace no matter what material possessions you had that proved you were doing "good" in this life. Material possessions are anything material or anything that has form that is possessed mentally by the ego and attempts to be used as proof that you are doing well in life because of it. These material possessions can include pretty much all things that the ego attempts to seek out in life from physical possessions to connections shared with other people that are considered extremely personal and rare even.

The connections that are experienced between two people, whether it is from mother to daughter, father to son, best friends, lovers, or anything that is considered unique or special based on past events, can also keep us trapped in the ego experience. It is hard to see this because these connections we seek out with others are the only extreme we have ever known from the awareness of birth. The ego seeks its definition in the accumulation of connections with others. Have you ever known someone who seeks to have a crazy number of friends? Or the opposite of that thought form, have you known anyone who seeks to only have a very select few "amazing" connections with certain friends? Unfortunately, these connections only point to some of the deepest attachments we can cling to in this life. When one of those attachments is taken away, suffering naturally follows.

To define your friendship as a great friendship is simply the ability to put someone else before yourself and to remain present for them no matter what drama is arising constantly. The unfortunate thing about this is it requires that something special or extra be applied to the thought of yourself and the connection you think you share with them. As you will see the "connection" is an illusion, but the ability to unconditionally love and accept another person by always putting their needs before your own is truly rare. Otherwise, every single person we know would be our best friend and there would no longer be any suffering like starvation in the world because every person on earth would be taken care of by someone else and their outward needs would always be met.

Hopefully, you can see that you are seeking to define yourself by your ability to take care of another person's needs before your own, therefore creating the egoic illusion that a special "connection" or "bond" has been created. However, this special connection can be shared with every person on earth if you can let go of the thought that it adds something to you or makes you something better because of it. Just like all things in life, this illusion only lasts as long as both parties are willing to keep the illusion alive, for the moment one of the people does something extremely selfish, the connection is severed and the reality that it was all experienced in the mind is readily known. For example, if your best friend is secretly sleeping with the person you are in a relationship with, do you believe that special connection was witnessed exactly and as deeply as your mental attachment to the thought-form was? On the other hand, are you able to see that the connection is only special as long as selfishness doesn't enter the picture? The ego attempts to give these certain thought forms more meaning and not only more meaning but also eternalness to these meanings. This connection is so deep and special that it will last forever. The ego-self finds comfort in the thought that deep connections are eternal, but obviously when the illusion is seen through and the reality that it was just another mind-dominated state of consciousness is known, suffering arises once again.

The other thing to watch out for is "rebounding." We have all heard this term and it is a great pointer to how quickly mind-dominated states can arise and subside. Just as one definition of who you are ends, another can arise based on instantly clinging to another person to make another addition to yourself that is "good" or produces happiness. Your mind rubber bands and attempts to leave the suffering of one mental attachment behind to replace it quickly with one you believe will produce pleasurable experiences. Ultimately, neither state of consciousness was better or worse than the other one. The only difference is your willingness to accept one and deny the other based on your egoic attachment to each of them. One produced a denial of the present moment and was labeled bad; therefore, it was quickly replaced with one that the ego calls good and accepts in the present moment. At any rate, your ability to experience life as good or bad is all going to come down to how you define yourself in the present moment. You can either accept the peacefulness of the present moment in any form it takes or deny the present moment which produces the experience of suffering.

Chapter 39

LIFE GOES ON

HAVE you ever had someone tell you that they will be miserable without you for the rest of their life, only to find out that they got married a few years later to the love of their life? Have you ever had someone convince you that your own life was going to be miserable without them, only to find a new person who took better care of you than the last person did? Have you ever had your favorite pet die and to curb your suffering, someone bought you another one immediately? The list could be endless as there are just as many examples in the mind that point to the state of consciousness where a loss is experienced that you never thought you would get over, only to find out that life goes on and time heals all. Have you ever thought you could never love another person the way you loved the last, only to find out that you ended up loving different things about the next person you share experiences with? The egoic life is in constant motion and it doesn't require things to be exactly as the last set of experiences, it only requires a continuation of a new set of experiences. Without new experiences to focus on, suffering in the past is the only thing you might witness. One thing always remains the same until the day the mind/body experience no longer serves you a purpose, LIFE GOES ON. The awareness of life never changes, even though the mind/body experience leads you to believe that your entire life has been full of completely different experiences. If you get right to the core of life, you will see that you have always been aware of it. The only thing that doesn't change is that the egoic life progresses, and so does the illusion that life is all about going from one thing to the next and growing or progressing in life.

For most people, the ability to find peace in the present moment eludes them because they are so wrapped up in going from one thing to the next that there is no gap between them. It is a life full of ups and downs, achievements or failures, but never once have they seen past the illusion to the eternalness of the ability to witness all of it. The most amazing thing is the ability to stop what you're doing at this very moment and realize that you actually can witness the world of form. Take a moment to look around you right now and see that you always could experience life. You might have been so wrapped up in all the different forms it takes that you never really might have known this. To the ego, it seems so silly to think that life is as simple as the ability to witness it because the ego is so heavily attached to "creating" a life to live that is experienced in the mind, that it misses the one that was always present. Life is the good and the bad all at once, but neither at the same time. There is more to life than what is experienced in the mind. You can think that your life is over, only to find that it never truly got started until you were willing to just let go and be free from the suffering of the ego. You can cling so heavily to all of the things in your life that are not working, or you can take the opportunity that the present moment always presents to you and just let go. Start anew at this moment and breathe new life into situations that constantly cause you suffering. There is nothing more you can do to change something that isn't working other than to let go of the mental attachment to it to create space to enter the present moment where that one little attachment to suffering does not exist. There is always a way to end the suffering because life goes on and it is only stagnant as long as there are mental attachments to past thought forms.

The ability to be free and live in the moment comes from either the full release of past attachments all at once, or it can come from the practice of releasing past attachments to the ego-self slowly. What is perceived by the ego to be different moments is the same one taking different forms for the rest of your human experience. The mind views it as being different because the structure of the mind is built on differences and extremes. The mind views life like a swinging pendulum, believing that being the pendulum and the extremes it swings to itself is life. Consciousness on the other hand is the ability to even witness such a concept as a pendulum in the first place, for without consciousness no pendulum exists.

Chapter 40

NEWTON'S LAW

Have you ever heard the theory, "*To every action, there is always an equal and opposite reaction*"? This is another great pointer to the mind-dominated state of consciousness. You will see that life is typically experienced as a direct response to the outward actions of others. If someone is nice to you, then you are in turn nice back. If someone is negative towards you, then automatically you are negative in return. It points to the mental attachment that is needed to believe that action from another person automatically causes the same reaction from you. How often do you find yourself being nice to someone who is negative towards you? The ego instantly reacts to negativity to defend its illusory self. Most of the time there is absolutely zero conscious thought given to the type of response, as it is almost instant and just as effortless on your part as the sun rising in the morning and setting in the evening.

The actions of others that are directed toward each of us are in turn their response to outward stimuli that are experienced during their day as well. As we all know, this stimulus consists of all the things in the mind/body experience such as the witnessing of feelings and emotions, the witnessing of all five senses of the body, and the witnessing of thoughts arising and subsiding, etc. If someone was treated with love and compassion, then they will in turn respond with the same love and compassion that was shown to them most of the time. If you show love and compassion and their heavy ego-self isn't capable of that in return at the moment, forgive them for they know not what they do. If someone was put down in an attempt to somehow diminish their sense of self, then they in turn will react in the same manner and attempt to do what was done to them. The problem here is these mental attachments to an ego-self are what cause the majority of all suffering on earth. If there was a negative action directed towards us, yet we needed no negative reaction in defense of an illusory self, hopefully, you can see how the action was witnessed as arising yet not reacted to, hence no suffering was experienced because it was allowed to arise and wasn't instantly given any mental egoic meaning. When there is no need to create a mental enemy in the present moment, the other person is left waiting for a negative reaction from you for the drama to continue to unfold. However, if none were to come, then how can the other person possibly continue if they have nothing in return to react to? You have got to always remember, that in the mind-dominated state of consciousness, there is always something of form arising and subsiding. If you were self-aware and witnessed something arising, ultimately you now have a choice to react as if that thought form was real, or to witness it arising and do nothing at which point it would subside and another thought form would arise to take its place. You must understand that nothing is eternal in the mind-dominated state of consciousness. Everything that exists in the mind will have a beginning and an end. Certain thought forms seem eternal, but only as long as our attachment to the thought forms remains intact.

Ultimately, when full self-awareness is present, only then is an action witnessed that requires no equal or opposite reaction. Newton's laws only exist in the mind, and it is only the mind that ultimately has movement to it. The deepest level of consciousness that is always found in the present moment requires no movement for there is no illusory self that needs a defense, let alone has a mental attachment in the form of caring what someone has said or done to us. It is this state of full self-awareness that is the only thing I know of that I would consider labeling as eternal. It is also the only thing that truly gives us the ability to show compassion for our most evil mind-created enemies. The spaciousness of self-awareness allows for the arising of undesirable actions to be witnessed, and once it is witnessed, it allows for the awareness of compassion to arise in the same instant when you can see another person's ego negatively fighting for survival.

The ego is always negative in defense of itself. You never see a person get punched in the face and immediately rush home to bake the attacker a cake. The ego never accepts negativity from others as something that just IS. The Isness of the present moment is always mistaken as some type of form that is directed squarely at your egoic attachment. It is never seen as a form that is arising and subsiding, instead, it is seen as a form that is directed solely at the core of your ego, which in turn requires an equal and opposite reaction to keep that illusory self fully together and intact. If the ego does not mount a defense, then the illusion of itself could slowly crumble and become diminished. A person could feel lost and confused or like the other person has won and you have lost the battle.

Physical altercations are a great pointer to this fact. If you have ever been in a fight with someone else, the mind perceives the outcome as a victory if you end up physically hurting the other person more than you feel you have been hurt. If you feel the fight was won, then a strengthening of the ego-self is experienced. If you feel you lost the fight, then a diminished ego is experienced. The victor can in his mind go on to claim the spoils of war as he feels he has just proven his worth to the world by hurting another person, and the loser is left feeling lost, lonely, and confused. However, neither realizes they both ultimately lost the self-awareness battle where no action, let alone a reaction, was ever needed to begin with. Both egos in this example continued to stay lost in the world of form, and neither was self-aware enough to deny the battle before it ever had a chance to go through the various levels of mental movements from starting as a thought form, then progressing to a verbal form by speaking your displeasure about someone, and then escalating mentally to the level of a physical form of actually assaulting them.

Hopefully, you can see in mind-dominated awareness that every action has an equal and opposite reaction is just pointing to both people being stuck in the ego experience, and in the ego experience there is never a winner or loser, there is only full awareness of the ego-self, and zero true self-awareness.

Whenever there is awareness of the ego-self, there will always be the awareness of suffering!

Chapter 41

PEACE

When living in the ego experience, hardly a moment goes by that truly feels peaceful. There is always something to do or something more to add or subtract to the present moment to make it better which usually floods our full awareness of life. It's only when you stop seeking yourself in the world of form and fully accept what is as it exists without needing to add or subtract anything of form to enjoy life more that you can be fully present. Peace is only truly found in the present moment and doesn't require things to be perfect or situations to go exactly as planned in the mind. Peace isn't always the opposite of war either. True inner peace has absolutely nothing to do with conflict as true inner peace has no opposite. The deepest level of true inner peace just IS. Peace that exists in the mind will always have an opposite. The peace that exists in the mind will always require a denial of a particular form to accept its opposite as peaceful. The mental peace that all of us experience is part of the ego experience, and that is why it comes and goes as situations or circumstances arise and subside, because anything that exists in the mind is never eternal. Just as one form arises in the mind, it eventually subsides in the mind, which in turn gives rise to a different form to take its place. This phenomenon of identifying oneself with the arising and subsiding of forms is what I call living in the ego.

The true inner peace that can only be experienced by being fully present in the moment requires you to exist in the moment perfectly as you are without giving in to the constant selfish urges and cravings of the ego. For example, have you ever hosted a holiday get-together at your house? Have you ever felt the pressure and stress demanded by the ego to produce a wonderful time for your family and friends? There is stress leading up to the preparation of the event from all the planning. There is stress during all the running around and shopping for the event even to the point that you just keep throwing things into your shopping cart that you think will somehow make the occasion just that much better, even if none of it was on your shopping list. There is stress the morning of when you are busy making your house perfect and making all of the food. There is constant frustration as things arise while you are trying so hard to concentrate on preparing your meal and timing it perfectly. If anybody has kids, then you know how stressful it is when they do something that doesn't fit perfectly into your egoic ideal of how they should be behaving on a holiday of all days. As you probably know from experience, the day continues like this until the meal is had, the conversations have ended, and the last person has left your house for the night. Now that the event is over, an entirely new series of selfish events take place. You started the day off demanding that everything be perfect for your event. Now you could be ending your day demanding that everything remain perfectly calm and peaceful because you are so tired and stressed out that you deserve to relax and be pampered the rest of the night.

The example I just used is a typical day of living in the ego or living in the mind where no true peace is experienced. Even after everyone has left, the selfishness of the ego is still fully active and if you do not receive the relaxation and pampering that your ego seeks, then you can feel justified for yelling and screaming at everybody around you, saying things like, "I just worked my ass off all day long, and now it is my turn to relax." Or, "I cooked all day, so you need to do all the dishes and clean up." The list of things that could be said at this point is endless, but hopefully, you can see what I'm pointing at. When you identify yourself with the particular outcome of an event, such as a holiday that you are hosting, then hopefully you can see that it doesn't truly add anything to you if the event received good reviews by your family or friends, nor would it take anything away from you if it turned out to be a nightmare. The additions and subtractions of the ego-self ultimately only exist in the mind.

Let me attempt to run you through the same day as it could have been experienced from the perspective of true self-awareness or presence. In this example, you wake up in the morning feeling free as a bird. You are not witnessing much stress from the thought of your day as the holiday is here and it just IS. You know full well what will be, will be, therefore you just accept things as they arise and subside without identifying yourself with the forms themselves. You go shopping and get whatever you need to get or even whatever you feel like getting this year that might be entirely different from last year because you know full well what is required to host a holiday as you have done it many times in the past. This year is no different, it's always the same thing taking on a different form perhaps with different food and even different people, but the concept is always the same. As you go to the checkout line you see another person rushing to cut in front of you. Instead of walking faster to cut them off and to make sure your cart is in line first, you offer to let them go first as you are aware that they are living in the ego and are feeling rushed and stressed out. At this point, you might have lost a few minutes of your day, but you certainly haven't lost your self-awareness as you are still existing in the present moment fully accepting it just as it is without needing to change anything for the better. As you return home and start your food preparation, your mind could be attempting to pull you in a hundred different directions from all the arising thought forms you're witnessing, but as you gently acknowledge the arising of them and remain non-reactive to them, just as fast as they arise, you will witness them beginning to subside and your attention fully returns to what you were doing before you almost lost your focus. At this point, if you were still fully present and your child came up to you and asked you for help, you would easily be able to stop what you are doing and help them knowing full well that you are not losing anything by doing so, only that your attention has fully subsided from cooking and instead the form of being present for your child has now arisen. As your presence is no longer needed by your children, you instinctively return to finish making the holiday dinner for your family and friends to enjoy. At this point, if everyone has arrived and is talking among themselves and having a good time, there is no sense of accomplishment as everything that is happening at that moment just IS as it IS. You are fully able to be present and living in the moment enjoying yourself while giving your full attention to a conversation without the feeling that you need to rush off to do something else.

If the evening were to take a dramatic turn and some people started to argue and everyone started to have a bad time, it still wouldn't be experienced any differently as you are still fully able to accept even that experience without the need to egoically react in defense of a self that ultimately is an illusion. If you were to witness negative emotions and instant reactions in defense of a conceptualized self that is hosting this important event, then you would have lost your self-awareness and the presence that is always there to be experienced would have been covered up by the ego experience and you could instinctively blame others for completely ruining your holiday. The entire day that was experienced as true peace could now easily have been washed away by the diminished egoic thoughts that instinctively arise when drama is witnessed and reacted negatively.

Hopefully, you can see the difference between these two examples and understand that even half of a single day in your entire life that was truly experienced in full self-awareness is better and truly more peaceful than an entire life spent living 24/7 in the ego experience.

Chapter 42

RELATIONSHIP PROBLEMS

Are you ever stuck suffering in a relationship constantly, yet you feel lots of love for the other person? Maybe you just don't understand why being with them sometimes hurts so much. Have you ever had things go good for a while where you thought things were great, only to instantly have everything go bad again and wonder why it got back to such a negative place so quickly to the point that the relationship could end based on one more word or hurtful thought out of their mouth? When things are good in the ego experience, that is usually when you are present in your relationship. Living in the moment with the other person is when you are not attaching anything mentally from the past to the current situation. You feel completely free to experience life as it is happening with them over the opposite experience which is living in the ego or the mind-dominated state of consciousness.

When you switch gears, the presence is lost, and something arises in the mind that triggers a negative attachment to the past to surface, problems that are not happening in the current moment can attempt to be made real in the mind by bringing them up and also by acting out the negativity accordingly. For example, if you and your partner are having a great time out on the town and you're enjoying a nice dinner and things couldn't possibly be going better, then you notice your partner looking at another person. Instantly all of these old mental attachments arise about trust or cheating or whatever it may be, and you react, and that one single negative thought is now brought to the surface in an attempt to be made real. The presence is gone and now you witness the mind deeper and deeper, and the deeper you go, the more negative your night is getting.

What was once a nice peaceful dinner has now turned into an argument where the other person doesn't even know what you are talking about, because you have attempted to create a false reality based on them looking at someone else. They could have just glanced over as something caught their eye, but it doesn't matter, because now they are being yelled at for all the negative thoughts they are witnessing in their mind and all of the negative history they have carried along with them for times like this during your entire relationship. So hopefully, you can see in this simple example how the only problems that ever truly exist in any relationship are those that are created by the witnessing of a negative mind. The person who has reacted to a passing thought form and clung to it in an attempt to make it real has now lost all presence and has fully attached themselves to their ego-self.

When your conscious awareness is fully attached to your ego-self, all of the things that were experienced from the past now have an opportunity to be brought up like they are somehow currently relevant when honestly, they are not. Who you were yesterday is not who you currently are, and who you currently are is all based on your current thinking which then gives you the direction where you will head tomorrow. So, to be at a nice dinner and all of a sudden you are getting yelled at for something you did a year ago that you are currently not doing is nothing more than the other person witnessing an egoic attachment fighting for survival. It doesn't mean anything, nor does it prove you are better than they are; therefore, it serves no purpose to be constantly brought up over and over again.

It all boils down to becoming aware of why you are reacting to thoughts as if they are an absolute reality when there is always an opposite existing at the same time. Thought forms arise and subside just like anything else in the ego experience.

They are not eternal, and the reason they don't last forever is that nothing in the mind/body experience lasts forever. They are one more thing you can witness arising and subsiding constantly and if you don't stop reacting to life long enough to understand the nature of thought forms, then you will believe all thought forms to be absolute reality and your life experience will sway around like the wind, blowing from one thought to the next to the next never having any solid foundation of presence to work with. Life will be a roller coaster for the person who is extremely emotional and who constantly reacts negatively to any thoughts that arise based on outward circumstances in any situation.

Chapter 43

QUESTION EVERYTHING

I READ a Chinese proverb that said, "Great doubts deep wisdom. Small doubts little wisdom." It is a great pointer to the fact that if you only take life for what it is on the surface or everything you have ever known and have accepted as absolute reality, you will only continue to know your fully conditioned ego-self, and you might never have the opportunity to get in touch with the deepest part of yourself which I consider to be the present moment or the self that ultimately has no self. If you never stop to question why thoughts arise in the mind, or how thoughts arise in the mind, then how are you completely convinced that every thought that arises comes from what you would consider to be "YOU"? If you just accept what flows into your awareness all day long without giving any thought to it, then you are just witnessing the egoic mind that consists of nothing but pleasurable thoughts arising every second to help you get through your day in the most pleasurable way possible. If you are a cup half-empty personality, then perhaps you experience negative thoughts which leaves you fully denying the present moment and stressing your way through your entire day. The importance of knowing this is not so much of what you are witnessing, but more importantly that you are reacting to the constant flow of thoughts arising in the egoic mind. The egoic lifestyle is that which avoids suffering, so a thought is witnessed and if it is pleasurable then it will be reacted to as if it is wanted. If it is a negative thought, then perhaps it is reacted to with some sort of avoidance or denial of the thought itself. Either way, there is a mental movement of some form that spawns a reaction of some type that somehow seeks to improve your mental positioning.

All of your thoughts that are arising are based on past mental conditioning from experiences that one might consider good or right, or even bad or wrong. Life can then be played out according to your surroundings and the interconnectedness of the world of form. For example, if you were born here in America, then perhaps your surroundings consist of a growth-oriented attitude, where schooling and a career is your biggest priority in life. If you grew up in some part of Africa or the Middle East somewhere, then perhaps the awareness of education and career doesn't even have the opportunity to arise because your entire life focus might be all about the avoidance of starvation and disease and day-to-day survival itself. Hopefully, that simple example gives some awareness to the fact that just because your surroundings support the opportunity to go to school and find a career that sustains you, doesn't make you a better person because your body is fed, and your life isn't a day-to-day struggle to survive. Unconditional love and compassion arise from knowing it is the same life, just a different form. I think each of us should take a good look at our lives and see how silly our dilemmas are. Most people in the world are living paycheck to paycheck to survive. How rough life is compared to someone who is living meal to meal where missing just one more meal could be the death of them?

I'm writing this book in hopes that to the people who can afford to buy a book, it might help them slow that narrow-minded egoic focus so that the selfishness of the ego diminishes, and the pleasure-seeking of the ego slows enough so that some space opens up for love and compassion for others to arise. If you don't stop to question anything in life, then you are stuck in the mental flow of it, and mainly your love and compassion are only reserved just for yourself or maybe a few others that you call family or friends.

Only when you begin to question why your entire life is built on pleasure-seeking, does space begin to open up in your conscious awareness that now allows room for new thoughts to arise that no longer consist of your selfish desires. When the intense laser beam-like focus is taken off your ego-self and the steady flow of jumping from one selfish mind movement to the next begins to slow, only then are you able to slowly return to the present moment where an infinite amount of spacious awareness is present. You no longer seek to insert your conceptualized ego-self into every possible pleasurable situation or perhaps growth-oriented opportunities, as you slowly become aware that the only self that truly attains pleasure or grows is the self that is conceptualized in the mind.

It is only when you have begun to question everything that new space arises in your consciousness and new realizations about yourself also arise. Without the questions arising, there is no need for answers to arise either. Without stopping the flow of the mind/body experience long enough to realize the space that is needed in your conscious awareness for you to find the answers that you seek has always been present, life will continue as normal from birth to death all the while playing out the storyline of the ego with no true self-awareness present to work from. The selfishness of the ego-self even if minimal to the point it is not readily apparent to others could still be taking up your entire conscious awareness. Selfishness doesn't always relate to a negative outward attitude that others pick up on. It usually just dominates your entire lifestyle without your awareness of it. It is a routine of pleasurable experiences that are constantly sought after. It can take the form of the simplest routine such as drinking a soda during every meal or even hanging out with friends every day. Helping others, if done for the wrong reasons, can be experienced as selfish desires being fulfilled. You will only know this when you go out of your way to help someone, and they don't give you the praise you were selfishly seeking in return. Ultimately, if you are adding something to yourself in some manner, then it is selfish. Selfishness is what sustains the ego because without it you would no longer enjoy the finer things in life, would you? If you let go of those routines of pleasure-seeking, what would your life look like and where would your happiness go?

Nothing of form should be exempt from questioning.

Start with small things like your desire to drink soda, then work your way up to the biggest things like mental attachment to love and your friends or family. Every form has an attachment to it. Question all of them from birth until the present moment to see how the attachment started and how it has solidified itself into the deepest attachments you have that will ultimately create the biggest amount of suffering for you like if a family member dies. It is the attachments that we hold the most near and dear to us that keep us from experiencing true self-awareness. If you are unwilling to question something like love, then how are you ever expecting to experience freedom from it? Most people don't want to question love because it feels good, but love is one of the biggest forms that cause the deepest suffering. Ask yourself how is it possible that when a family member dies you are destroyed, but you hear about ten people who die on the local news every day without giving it another thought. Mental attachment is one of the biggest obstacles to releasing the ego. The illusions that have attachments are what create our reality whereas illusions that are just witnessed and not clung to are simply experienced as white noise. The important part of questioning everything is to understand what mental attachment is and how your entire reality is based on the total of these attachments which I refer to as ego. Why do you believe all of the things you do about life and yourself? Why does your ego fight for survival when any of these beliefs are challenged and what are you afraid of if you let go of them to see the truth? I can guarantee the truth is nothing like you thought it was as seeing behind the curtain of life IS the awareness of all of the illusions that you consider life to be in the first place. Life is in its purest form awareness itself. Question what has made your life the way it is and then work backward to let go of all of the forms to find out who you are without them.

Eventually, there will be nothing of form left and you will simply exist as nothingness surrounded by the awareness of the world of form knowing you are something greater than form itself, yet you do not depend on form to exist. That, my friends, is in my opinion, enlightenment! The awareness of the formless self that never needed a self to exist.

Chapter 44

EGO AND RETALIATION

In the ego experience when somebody wrongs you in some fashion, there is always a need or even a pull towards getting them back somehow. Does the punishment need to fit the crime? Or does the egoic desire to make them suffer win out where you do something just a little bit more than they did to you? The ego is all about adding or subtracting something to the present moment, so retaliation in any form will always fit in either category. An easy example would be experiencing constant anger over your neighbor's dog going to the bathroom in your yard. Let's say you have confronted the neighbor and asked them to pick up the dog poop, but they just blow it off like it's no big deal. Instinctively, the ego is now pulling you in the direction of making them suffer as you have been suffering. You might grab a shovel and begin flinging the dog poop back into your neighbor's yard. Or maybe you throw it on their car or house. The more you lose your self-awareness in the present moment the more negative things you might begin to do towards them in an attempt to prove your suffering.

When the neighbor confronts you about all of the dog poop on their car or even their house, your only explanation would be something along the lines of, "Well I asked you to clean it up and you wouldn't, so you deserved it." This little example that can take on a multitude of different scenarios is an addition to the present moment, meaning more form is being added. If you were to do the opposite and subtract something of form from the neighbor, then perhaps you would go as far as to abduct his dog and drop it off in a different city. Instead of the neighbor coming home and finding something added to the present moment, like dog poop on his stuff, he might experience a subtraction of form as in a missing dog, and experience suffering that way. Either way, retaliation of any kind is an act of pure selfishness and should be avoided if you are self-aware enough to do so.

You will see that the longer you are engaged in an egoic battle with your neighbor, the violence level might steadily increase. What was once just a simple annoyance of having dog poop in your yard could have easily escalated to theft, or even slashing their tires out of anger. It could lead to physical violence to full-on murder, depending on how deeply you have lost touch with the present moment and attempted to find yourself in the anger that is witnessed in the mind. The ability to remain present and self-aware is the only thing that could have stopped all of this anger and violence before it ever was witnessed and acted upon. The moment your ego was challenged by your neighbor's unwillingness to accept your suffering as real, is the moment you should have seen your ego beginning to dominate your awareness. If there is zero self-awareness present, then the situation will continue to unfold until one person has claimed to be the victor and the other person has either admitted defeat or was self-aware in the first place to deny the battle before it ever had an opportunity to continue to take form.

Ultimately, do you win by causing your neighbor suffering, or do they win by inflicting more suffering on you? How much suffering is enough to consider it an egoic win, and did a single thought ever arise that could have stopped the cycle of suffering before it ever began? Would the neighbor have lost anything by picking up after their dog, to begin with, to avoid any further problems? Would you have lost anything by picking up after your neighbor's dog even if your neighbor refused to? Why is it not acceptable for dog poop in your yard to arise ever unless it's your own dog's poop? These are all questions that the ego can easily answer because the ego always has an enemy. That enemy is considered the present moment or the opposite of doing nothing or thinking nothing. The ego doesn't want to just exist without needing anything of form since the entire illusion of the ego is based solely on the combination of different forms. Would you still want to retaliate against anything in life if you did not have emotions? Would you still want to retaliate against anything in life if you did not have thoughts? Would you still want to retaliate against anything in life if you did not have a physical body? These are all questions that the ego cannot easily answer as the ego is an illusion based on form, so it has no awareness of the formlessness of consciousness. If you start asking the deeper questions from the context of full self-awareness, then hopefully, the ego will dissolve enough for a greater understanding of the present moment to emerge where nothing needs to be added or taken away from the present moment as everything is perfect and complete the way it is currently experienced. As always, life is the same thing taking on a different form.

Chapter 45

SOCIAL NETWORKING

ANOTHER POINTER to the ego experience and why it is so important to have awareness of it can be seen in all of the successful social networking websites as they are designed to capture your attention. It is very easy to lose your self-awareness by feeling the need to constantly check to see if anybody has responded to your messages or to play the games that require you to check back every few hours to maintain the illusion that you are working towards something. When you post a daily quote and constantly check back to see if anybody likes it or has commented on it, the ego attachment is pulling your attention back because you have to know what's next. The ego needs a constant continuation of the human experience. That need or that pull to check the website is the ego experience. If you can catch yourself as that desire arises, stop before you look, and realize that you don't need to. It is the ego experience that demands that you look and continue commenting, playing your game, or searching for new friends. The ego is all about the constant addition and subtraction of form. That feeling of frustration or disconnectedness that is experienced when the power goes out and you can't use your computer is the ego experience. When you feel the way you do when you have designed your farm or city while playing those games, it is a direct reflection of you. Then you have lost your self-awareness. You are ego-identified with the creativity that has arisen in the present moment. You feel that creativity has come directly from you, instead of realizing that creativity is simply just creativity arising in the present moment. If you are constantly posting new pictures of yourself doing every new experience, then hopefully you can see how you are trying to create a storyline of how enjoyable and exciting your life is or maybe how sexy you believe yourself to be.

The opposite of these examples would be to still do them but to not lose yourself in them. You can still post pictures connect with friends and play these games, but as long as you are aware that this is all something that you do, not something that you are, then you can remain self-aware while doing them. If someone was to take the internet completely away from you and you just don't think you could go on living anymore, then you are heavily ego-attached. If your ego is finding itself in something that you just can't live without, then there is still plenty of work to be done. If you are still using the various forms that are out there for entertainment without egoic desires leading to suffering if you lose them, then you are doing pretty well. Keep in mind that cell phones act the same way as social networking websites. You probably know more people who are glued to their cell over their computer, but the egoic attachment can still be experienced the same way. You witness a need of some sort arising, such as text messaging friends, and then you must be able to keep in constant contact to not experience suffering. You need the comfort that is experienced in the idea of being connected to others somehow. You need your cell phone to maintain your business or your friendships. No matter what it is, without a social connection, you might experience suffering. In the end, as always, no matter if it is cell phones or computers on the internet, the ego attachment is always the same thing taking on a different form.

Chapter 46

SEEKING LIFE

In the ego experience, the attainment of a better life is usually the only awareness that dominates each of our human experiences. People tend to seek a perfect life through relationships, careers, or social activities. The problem is when you seek life outwardly, you completely disregard the awareness of the present moment. You are stuck living a life in your mind. This is what I call the mind-dominated state of consciousness. The awareness of moving from one thing to the next, to the next, all the way until death is a typical human experience. The pursuit of something bigger, better, or greater always looms in the background as the driving force and is usually the context in which all people hold the concept of life. Not many people are happy if they feel they are lacking something. They believe their happiness is always going to be found in the next best thing, so they continue to seek life outwardly.

The problem is that in the world of form, everything that arises will always inevitably subside. Absolutely nothing in the world of form is eternal. All of the forms that exist from physical forms, to emotional forms, to mental forms all have a shelf life.

They are only temporary even if they seem permanent in the mind.

Relationships even if maintained for sixty years have an ending when one of the people involved passes away. Emotional forms such as the extreme sadness that is experienced when someone cheats on you and the relationship ends swiftly and unexpectedly have an ending when you finally let go or find someone else. Even mental forms such as the horrific mental concepts that Adolf Hitler spread during his time as the chancellor of Germany between the years 1933 and 1945 had an ending. Hopefully, with the example of Adolf Hitler alone, you can see that the attainment of a perfect life that is sought through form has the potential to lead to tremendous suffering.

As more things of form are added to life the more it can seem exciting and fresh and new and somehow different than it was. This is what gives rise to the illusion that having more or becoming more is a real and eternal thing. Ultimately, it is just another way for your ego to seek itself and to fight for survival in the world of form. You will know it is not real or eternal the moment you lose everything you have worked for, and suffering is experienced. It is always the shifting of form that makes one aspect of life seem different from another as there is always another mental form that can rise and take the place of the previous egoic form that has subsided. As one idea of a career subsides and another different form arises that seems better is experienced, you naturally feel some progress in life is made after the mental attachment to suffering over the loss of the first job is experienced. You feel you are somehow a better person now that something better has happened to you.

Bouncing from one egoic form to the next that is considered better is what leads to mental security or the idea that you are doing good in life. No attention is paid to the fact that you suffered as you lost your first job until you found another one that you considered better. The mental suffering arises because there is no allowance for forms to subside unless it is on your terms. When an illusion crumbles and you didn't choose for it to happen, you suffer. When an illusion is released for another illusion to take its place and you feel you made the right choice based on progress in life, then you can see how you have only avoided suffering as long as the change was on your terms. The rest of life is experienced this way as well. Avoid suffering to seek a better life.

There is nothing wrong with avoiding suffering, but the moment you close yourself off to the notion that suffering isn't allowed to happen to you is the moment you deny the present moment in any form that it takes. You end up stuck living in your mind doing all different kinds of things to avoid suffering in any form it takes. This is ultimately the root of all selfishness. The avoidance of suffering is what leads people to take advantage of other people. To put their own needs before another person's needs. It can lead to murdering another person to avoid suffering as you see all the time on TV when a robber shoots the victims to avoid leaving witnesses behind that might be able to put him in jail. The list is endless, but no matter what form the avoidance of suffering takes, it is all a denial of the present moment. The interconnectedness of form is what gives rise to each particular conceptualized form. For example, when you add the form of a person who is attempting to avoid financial suffering by the willingness to steal from others with the form of a ski mask and a gun, then the interconnectedness of those things adds together and gives rise to an armed robber.

Even though people who seek life in form only find suffering in the end, it can be an exciting process until the illusion is seen through. Just as the person who is seeking advancement in the workplace experiences excitement, so does the armed robber when they witness the thought of adding something better to the present moment. That excitement is what keeps people constantly seeking life through different avenues of the ego. The addition of form is all an attempt of the ego to grow and define itself as something more than it was previously. So, the attainment of a perfect life is usually sought outward in any concept that exists in the mind. It can be good/bad, right/wrong, positive/negative, one person can add something that another person would never add to the present moment, the only difference is what you're witnessing arising in the mind at the time. One person can seek to help all others while another chooses to harm all others. We live in a world of opposites and that is what gives rise to the notion of right and wrong, good or bad, this or that. You just simply need to see that no matter what form or definition is given to what you are seeking yourself in, it is the same for every person on earth, it just seems completely different based on the form it takes.

It is this seeking of something that we call life that leaves all of us blind to the present moment where true peace can be found no matter what life situation we are experiencing. This outward-looking for something better or the doing-ness of life is what covers up the consciousness that is present in all of us. The mind-dominated state of consciousness has a constant motion to it and if you're stuck seeking something, you will never truly be found. You will never touch the present moment deeply enough to become aware of the non-reaction or unconditional love and acceptance that is present in every single human on earth. It is our natural state of being. It is the foundation that the entire world of form rests on. It is the key to the end of all human suffering, and it has always existed perfectly as it is in its dormant state just waiting for each of us to return to the present moment which is the only place it can be experienced.

The best way to return to your innocence is to just stay present and grounded in the here and now. It is so easy to get swept up in everything that the world of form has to offer that we simply forget who we are at the core of our being. Even the concept of BEING isn't accurate as a being implies that it has a container or all of these things that are put together to form a self when ultimately consciousness has no container or outline that defines it as separate from being one with everything that exists. There is no being somewhere existing separate from what you already are at this moment. We just get so caught up in the storyline of me that it seems like we need to add all of the knowledge learned in this life to form a being that we call ME or I. This pursuit of self-awareness through form is why it is not so easy to just start a spiritual journey and that is enough and all of a sudden you become self-realized. Searching through anything of form to find yourself is a lost cause; it is an endless maze. The only place you can find yourself is in the present moment RIGHT NOW, in every thought, every action, every reaction. Question WHY you react to every single thing the way you do and with enough practice of bringing your awareness back to this very second and maintaining it right here, right now, you will find the root of your consciousness and in doing so you will finally be able to see every single person on earth as the same thing you are only taking on a different form!

Chapter 47

THE ART OF NON-REACTION

IN THE EGO EXPERIENCE, non-reaction doesn't even exist. The ego loves to instantly react before your conscious awareness even has the opportunity to decide what you want to experience in the present moment. You will see this in all areas of your life from relationships to your job to dealing with your children or family. Just as quickly as something new arises, there is an instant reaction to it. If your spouse yells at you, then you instantly react. If your boss at work yells at you, then you instantly react even if you don't say anything out loud. If your child breaks a window in your house, then you instantly react. If your mother, father, or family members are constantly telling you how to live your life, then you are constantly reacting to that.

The form of the reaction is not important as it takes on the form that it takes in the moment from reacting physically, emotionally, or mentally. How many times has someone yelled at you and you just smiled and stood there perfectly at peace and tranquil? Probably not many. For most of us when someone is directing anger at us, we experience some form of physical feelings in our stomach, or we instantly feel extremely defensive or we completely disregard everything they are saying because in our mind we are thinking we are better than them and they know nothing therefore it might not make you feel anything other than annoyed. Nonetheless, all of those examples are reactions to form arising. In the case of someone yelling at you, it can be considered a thought form. The other person has an idea in their head, and they direct that idea in the form of yelling that idea at you. They could say, "You don't have a job, so you are worthless." Or, "You're the reason my life is horrible and that's why I am leaving you." No matter what concept they witness arising, the ego always needs to direct it at someone or something. This is how a mental enemy is born. The ego completely denies the present moment and a reaction to that denial is experienced. It might have been yelling one minute and then it passes, then it might arise again two days later in the form of name-calling. The denial could be so heavily clung to that you could still quite possibly hate a childhood friend that you feel did you wrong to this day even if they are not even in your life anymore. There are no limits to how long you choose to hold a grudge, but it is only when you begin to accept the present moment that the grudge begins to diminish. The negative thoughts or feelings are just illusions, all you have done is deny the present moment in the form it took at the time and call it reality. You reacted instantly to a form arising and responded accordingly based on your egoic ideals as to what you considered right or wrong at the time. This conceptualized mentality can lead us to a lifetime of suffering if we are not willing to learn how non-reaction or full acceptance of the present moment can save us from potentially never experiencing being a victor and always being a victim. Someone who has attained mastery over the present moment can consider that a victory while someone who only knows how to deny the present moment might consider themselves a victim for the rest of their life. The victim mentality has no peace attached to it. It only knows suffering and sees it at every bend in the road. They live a life of constant roadblocks. The only peace they might find could be in the punishment of those whom they feel have wronged them, but even that peace that might initially be experienced will also pass.

The art of non-reaction is simply the ability to see the world through unconditional eyes. There is no good or bad, right or wrong placed on every single thing that arises. You -simply fully accept that just as truly wonderful and amazing things happen so too can truly horrible things. You accept this only after you have the awareness that both extremes of the mind exist at the same time. Without this awareness then it's understandable that you might never want to fully accept something truly horrible that happens to you. Nonetheless, the only control you have is the illusion of control that exists in the mind. You might try to think about non-reaction as the ocean. The waves consist of reactions to the world around us that constantly arise and subside, a wave goes up, a wave goes down, one wave is big, and another one is small. The waves happen on a superficial level where the ego exists, where non-reaction is the water itself. The water itself knows some waves come and go yet it is perfectly content existing in stillness just as it is, knowing that everything that happens on the surface is simply witnessed as the world of form arising and subsiding constantly. Ultimately, the water itself cannot stop the waves from happening as it is only the witness, just as we cannot stop all the horrible things in the world from happening to us. The only thing we can ever truly control is how we react to the world of form as it is arising and subsiding in our lives. We might not be able to stop someone from murdering a friend or family member, but if we become aware of the art of non-reaction, then we can stop ourselves from possibly murdering someone else's friend or family member by not losing control in the present moment.

If we become aware that suffering only exists in the mind, then we can also become aware that the end of suffering is through non-reaction in the present moment. It is not the fact that we force ourselves not to suffer when something terrible happens as that would be more denial of the present moment. When true non-reaction is experienced, we witness the arising of the form of suffering and we no longer instantly react to that form, which in turn allows it to subside. When we create a mind-dominated self that avoids form by showing no emotions, then the ego has just created another form of itself that is somehow better than a person who shows uncontrollable emotions when suffering arises.

It is through this non-reactive state of consciousness that the most amazing and loving things have the opportunity to arise. It's not thinking that serving the homeless at a soup kitchen on the weekend would look good on a resume because that is pure egoic thinking, but the true presence or non-reaction is where you can truly help others from a place that has zero selfishness attached to it. There is no longer a need to gain something or to keep up the illusion that you are something or someone who helps others. The ego cannot exist in a place where something isn't added to it as the ego's biggest defense is its ability to shift forms to fight for survival.

A good example of the egoless state of awareness is Mother Teresa's ability to help people who nobody else wanted to help. She would encounter the most down-and-out people in the world who were lying on the street dying with absolutely nothing to give her in return. She would pick them up and bring them in and offer them the very necessities of life, the most important besides food and water being unconditional love and acceptance. She did not view them as diminishing her somehow. Instead, she saw them as the same thing as she was only taking on a different form. In the context in which she held life, it could have been that she saw them as the most holy child of God, just as she saw herself. No matter what context she believed, she was self-aware and present enough to save a life that nobody else considered valuable. She could recognize the eternal essence that was present in them, the same essence that is present in all of us, only she put their needs before her own and offered them a second chance at experiencing the world of form when the world of form or other people's egos didn't.

Ultimately, what she did made her good in the eyes of the others. It made her a saint, even though she didn't need the credit. All she did was to accept the present moment in the form it took and to tackle it from that non-reactive state of awareness. The peace that was found in that non-reactive state was able to save countless lives and we all can work from that state of awareness right now. She did what she did right from home, she didn't have to journey around the world to find suffering to fix like the ego might attempt to do. She took what was right in front of her and put the needs of others before her own. Each of us can do the same thing in our lives right now in this very moment. You don't need to go to the extreme and sell off all of your belongings and travel to a different country full of severe suffering. If we were to all just make a slight change to put the needs of others before our own as it arises in our daily lives with the people around us, that kind of presence can spread all across the world. It can spread from here at home, from one person to the next across the globe to the people who need it the most. We just need to give up thinking that we can't help or change the world because we do. It is only found right now in the present moment. You can be the change in the world that you seek, you simply just need to start by bringing your awareness of self to the present and away from the egoic state of consciousness. Just like throwing a pebble in a pond creates ripples, those ripples will spread across the entire pond to reach the far shore. The power of non-reaction has the same ability. If someone wrongs you, and you feel like you instantly need to react in retaliation, DON'T. If someone yells at you and you instantly feel the need to yell back to defend yourself, DON'T. This tiny bit of non-reaction might not seem like much, but you are single-handedly putting a stop to the motion of the ego. When others see how much you have changed and how peaceful you experience life through non-reaction, they will in turn also want that, and just by being the change you seek in the world, you will have done your part to make it a better place.

Mother Teresa, who when asked once how she had accomplished such great things in her life responded, "None of us can do anything great on our own, but we can all do a small thing with great love." She was pointing to the fact that doing something on your own is the egoic state or disconnected state with life. The tiny change we can all make which in turn can produce great things is the state of self-awareness. It may have taken the form of saving lives for her, but it can be a different form for each of us. Just one single time you choose non-reaction over instantly reacting to some form of negativity, and you have already made the world a better place. Let it spread by teaching others something they may have forgotten but has been right there right now waiting to be reclaimed or remembered. The presence that was in Jesus, Buddha, or Mother Teresa is also in you! Just because someone else isn't playing along with your non-reaction and they might consider you weak, or worthless for not standing up for yourself is only another reason to practice it more. Non-reaction doesn't have to mean standing there in silence after they yell at you. It means that your self-awareness is so strong that you no longer need to react to their words negatively. You can choose to accept their opinion and offer a positive one of your own instead of yelling more negativity back at them. When you see their ego fighting for survival by putting you down or attempting to diminish your ego by making fun of your non-reaction, instead of anger let that awareness of the ego that is present in them strengthen your resolve to continue to practice unconditional love and acceptance for all others. Be the miracle that this world desperately needs and shed that ego attachment because the non-reactive or enlightened state of being all starts with you right here right now in this very moment. You might have never had any experiences with non-reaction before, but you will always have the ability to practice it in this moment for the rest of your life! There is no perfect time to start or no particular circumstance that needs to arise before you try it, you simply just need to take it for a test drive and witness how good it feels to remain peaceful and non-reactive.

Chapter 48

———————

SHIFTING MENTAL PATTERNS

WHEN YOU ARE LIVING in the ego experience, your mental patterns can shift as frequently as the weather. You might feel a sense of needing something different or something that appeals to your false sense of self and its beliefs as to how you will be able to maintain some sort of progress in your life. You may feel you need to stop talking to certain friends to somehow be better, or you might feel that you all of a sudden need to end your current relationship because you need to be free to change or improve your life. The examples you can use to see this are as numerous as the stars in the sky, but the pattern is always the same. There is a need or want or some form of desire arising in your mind where you are willing to give something up that you see as lesser to gain something your ego sees as greater.

The mind and its shifting movements are constantly in motion and have been since birth, but when the ego continues throughout life to construct its storyline of me, it uses that which is witnessed arising at any given time as an excuse to pursue another aspect or greater version of itself. The continuation of the ego experience has another piece of the puzzle to use and another way to define itself at the given time, yet it still is simply one more illusion that is added to the mix and called ME. Time and time again when a certain amount of time has passed and the illusion is seen through, you are usually left wondering why you made such choices, almost as if you didn't know what you were doing at the time. When the self-awareness begins to set back in as the ego-self diminishes it is only then that you can see that you usually made the wrong choice.

It might have taken a few months or maybe a few years to realize that ditching out on a really good friend of yours at the time was not needed and when self-awareness arises to this fact you will see that the only true change happened within yourself. You will probably realize that having certain people in your life doesn't make or break you, it is your reaction to life at the time that truly has given you either a sense of accomplishment or a sense of failure. When you deny a person that you consider to be a friend or a lover because you feel they are a bad influence, for example, you are only denying your inner desires. Instead of taking responsibility for those desires that are arising, ultimately you are only denying the form of the person that you have created in your mind. You are not coming to terms with your desires but are instead choosing to deny the present moment in the form your friend or lover has taken in your mind out of fear that it will lead to something you don't want to do or experience anymore.

The ability to deny someone in this way stems from these shifting mental patterns and they usually directly relate to how your ego feels you are better than them in some way, shape, or form. You might think you are better like you have more going for you, or that you are good, and they are bad for you and will only bring you down with them, etc. Each of those thoughts is just more shifting mental patterns based on what is arising in the present moment at the time you witness them. The interconnectedness of everything at the time is what gives rise to these thoughts. You could have been hanging out with them every day for the past five years drinking or doing drugs with them without witnessing one little thought arise about seeing anything wrong with what you are both doing, yet the moment you decide to quit, and they don't, you automatically witness the need to get better than them. You begin to witness a departure from this old ego-self that was perfectly fine with being their friend, to this new and improved version that is now trying to be better than they are so naturally you must get away from them to have the freedom to be a better person.

The problem with living your life based on these shifting mental patterns is they never end. Your entire life will be spent chasing one better thought after another. You could spend your entire life denying the present moment to progress in the ego experience chasing down illusions. You could also wake up one day and wonder why you are all alone and why people don't choose to be around you when you feel you have done so well for yourself that people would be stupid not to be jealous of what you have. The most basic principle of the ego experience is growth and there is nothing wrong with growth if it is done out of self-awareness. If you were self-aware, you would no longer need to deny your friends no matter what form they take as you are able and willing to love them unconditionally. No matter what is happening around you or to you, there is always a peaceful spaciousness that can be your haven from the world of form. It is only when you react to the shifting mental patterns that constantly arise that we ever find ourselves out of sync with the present moment and fully living in the shadow of the ego.

Chapter 49

OUT OF CONTROL

IN THE EGO EXPERIENCE, we have all had times in our lives when things have been completely out of our control. We have witnessed events arising that we didn't wish to witness, we have lost loved ones that we didn't want to lose, and we have even done things we didn't know had any consequences until after the fact. For most of us, the total of our lives has consisted solely of constant reactions to the world of form. We have all tried our best to keep good forms in our lives constant, yet no matter how hard we try forms that we consider negative will always arise just as quickly. Maybe you got pulled over and your friend who was your passenger got scared and stuffed his drugs in your seat; maybe that led to the cops finding it and you ended up in jail. Maybe you were driving your car home from work and a drunk driver hit you head-on and put you in the hospital, or maybe it happened to your spouse, and they died from their injuries.

The constant arising and subsiding of form brings with it the ability for anything that is contained in the mind to happen to you at any given time. Every single possible thing that has ever been known or will ever be known that has been stuffed into a container called the mind can arise at any moment for no reason whatsoever. In the Bible, it says that the rain falls on the just and unjust alike. This teaching is pointing at the fact that the world of form does not discriminate as one might hope. You could have spent your entire life being what you considered to be good or even holy and still witness horrible things happen to you or your loved ones. It is only when we begin to accept this reality that our suffering begins to diminish. Only after full acceptance and awareness, that the world of form is in a constant state of change are we free from the sufferings of the arising and subsiding of certain forms. The lack of control is freedom from suffering, whereas the clinging to the illusion of control is what causes suffering the most. It is the things we cannot change and the egoic desires to constantly change things that leave us hurting so much in the end.

If we need a reason as to why something has happened, that is the first sign that we are still stuck in the ego experience. If we can accept that there is no reason as to why one form arises or another form subsides as that is simply the way the mind/body experience operates, then we can experience peace with all arisings and subsiding of form. As your self-awareness grows, and I wouldn't even call it growth as it is quite the opposite, but as it shrinks itself from the awareness of the mind-dominated state of consciousness back-tracking through the world of mental form until it reaches your natural state of being or the present moment where nothing is added, you begin to experience the arising of inner peace. This is also why it is so important to live as presently as possible, especially with your loved ones as they too have a physical form that will someday no longer serve them a purpose and will subside as well even before you would consider it their time to go. When you reach a level of self-awareness that fully mind-dominated people might consider cold-hearted about loss, you can use that as another pointer that you can see mental attachment and the awareness of form for what it truly is and even if they can't believe how you are not suffering so terribly like they are, you won't hold it against them for they are only aware of the sufferings of the ego. Peace is a freedom that is only found in the present moment. The more compassion you show others, the more they will allow you to help them return to the present moment. Unfortunately, exposing their inability to allow things to exist just as they are without needing to control them during times of loss might not be the best idea as the ego fights fiercely for survival when confronted with the notion of physical death. I have seen the ego blame others for not loving someone as much as they did and to prove it the person made a big scene and told off a sibling in front of everyone and it took years before the person yelling regained enough self-awareness to let their sibling back in their life. So just as the example of a dying person who lacks control on your part, so does the shifting mental movements of another person. You might never have wanted a sibling to be mad at you for five years, but that too is out of your control. The more spaciousness you give the other person for them to return to a self-aware state of being the better. The more you fight for control by attempting to tell the other person they were wrong, the more they remain in that mind-dominated state of I am right, and you are wrong. In the end, you can hopefully see that the more attachments you release in all areas of your life the less suffering you will experience.

Chapter 50

PEACEFUL SILENCE

I HAD a person ask me the other day if sitting in silence was living in the present moment. I noticed he was witnessing a thought arising as I could see him trying to elaborate on the thought that sitting in silence was the only place where he found peace. He explained how he had been trying so hard to live presently that he would hurry home from work, shut off his cell phone, and lock himself in his office for a few hours away from his wife and kids just sitting silently. I tried to explain to him that what he was doing was just another form of the ego experience. Even though that particular form simulated presence it was ultimately just another mind-dominated illusion. I tried to point out that what he was doing was denying the present moment by hurrying home from work, disconnecting himself from others by shutting his cell phone off, and then denying his family time with his wife and kids so that he could push away the world of form to sit in silence. I also tried to explain that the current moment has his wife and children present in it and that he should fully accept when that arises and enjoy his time with them and sit in silence when he is home alone instead. Unfortunately, he was not living presently at all, as he was at the very least denying his wife and children, which caused them suffering by ignoring them to sit alone in silence. Although sitting in silence to gain presence is a good concept, I don't quite think he realized that his presence depended on silence. There was still a "this" causing a "that." His peacefulness depended on absolute silence and whenever something depends on something else to exist, that is still an illusion of the ego experience as suffering still arises when the opposite happens. When his children would make loud noises, he would yell to make them quiet. When his dog scratched at his door, he said he would get angry as it broke his concentration. The arising of suffering is still pointing at the fact that he has not fully accepted the present moment yet even though it has taken the form of something peaceful like sitting in silence.

True peace is always present with you no matter if you are at a rock concert, or sitting in the stands at a NASCAR race where you can't even hear yourself think. It can be experienced while you are spending time with your wife and kids, or it can also exist while you are driving home from work in rush hour traffic or talking on your cell phone. No matter what form arises outwardly, when you tap into the true peace of the present moment it is always available to you. It is nothing you have to seek, for it already is the core of your being. You don't need to sit in a cave in Tibet for years to find it any more than you need to read a book to learn how to meditate to experience it.

Sitting in silence can be a great pointer, especially to understanding the nature of the mind. When you are alone in silence with your eyes closed what do you have left to witness except the mind? Question why you are sitting there trying to be silent when the mind is busy singing a song, or going over a grocery list, or thinking about errands you have to run still. Then realize you could have worked your way through all of those thoughts while you were busy playing with your kids. I think one of the biggest illusions about spirituality is that you need to act a certain way or do certain spiritual things to receive the gift of spiritual enlightenment or self-realization.

The simple fact is the self you are seeking has always been present with you throughout your entire life no matter what you were doing. It is the eternal well of stillness from which all forms arise. It never required that you sit still or sit in silence to drink from that well, it was already the well you have experienced your entire life to begin with. It was just covered up with your inability to witness anything except the nature of the mind! You never once needed to meditate or chant for eighteen hours a day to become aware of it. Those forms are designed to help you push away other forms and to learn to become focused on one single form, because as the mind and body are fully engaged in an activity the less you cling to them as being you. When you fully let go of them you will see that they will continue to do their thing all on their own and all of a sudden consciousness in the form of the present moment will arise and you will for the first time become aware of a new dimension of presence that was always there, it was just covered up by the mind/body experience. The more you bring attention to the awareness of the peace and stillness that exists every second of every day as you are living your life fully the better. You don't need to sell off your worldly possessions to rush off and join a monastery to learn how to touch the present moment. Even though it seems easier to do that, even a monastery still has a form to it and it could be very easy to lose yourself in that form just as easily as it was with the form your life took that you just sold off and left behind.

My advice to him was to continue living the daily life that was arising for him in this moment and to simply bring awareness back to the present moment by just being there for his family. Presence means being grounded in everything you do. I told him to stop living in the future by working so hard trying to provide a good life for his wife and kids to the point where it was his entire life focus. He kind of forgot that he had an obligation to them other than to provide for them financially. I tried to remind him that children remember how many times you were present enough to help them with their homework over how much money you had in the bank at the time. I tried to help him learn that providing a good life for his wife and kids was a life that is lived with them instead of living one in the mind always stressed out about the future. To live presently is to find a balance between your work time and your family time. One must be present with their family to truly live a life with them, otherwise, you could end up working all the time attempting to provide this hugely amazing life that you have created in your mind. The problem with living in the mind is that is where opposites exist, so even though you might think you are a huge success, your spouse and your children might think you are a huge failure, because they feel they are living alone.

There is another side to this coin as well. I tried to explain that if sitting in silence was helping him to find more peace in his life, then he should take some time for himself to do that as well as long as it wasn't causing anybody suffering.

Existing peacefully and neglecting others might seem like two different things, but the same form of sitting in silence can produce two different experiences if they are not done the right way at the right time. I explained the importance of being present enough to catch himself before he yelled at his kids to be quiet or before anger was allowed to arise when the dog scratched his door. I tried to show him that bringing awareness to things of that nature is a true presence. Learn to accept that the ego is programmed to instantly react and if your conscious awareness is present before that reaction occurs then you will have a choice on how to react the way you truly want to instead of the way your ego is programmed to. This awareness of the arising of the ego response to outward stimuli is what you need to bring your full attention to. Sitting in silence is just sitting in silence, but to live presently enough to choose how to react to life each second of the day is living a truly present life that is void of suffering as you won't automatically suffer unless you choose to.

Chapter 51

COMMUNICATION

IN THE EGO EXPERIENCE, even some of the most basic aspects of being human are all about progressing the mind-dominated state of consciousness. Take communication for instance. When you talk to someone, you are expressing through speech the storyline of the ego. Without one thought going to the next and then to the next, how are you able to properly communicate exactly what you were thinking at the time when you are telling someone else a story? Have you ever noticed how when you tell a story you are communicating the experience exactly as it unfolded mentally? Without this awareness of why a story ends up being a story, then you are simply stuck in the ego just explaining another aspect of it as it arose. The ego is all about communicating its own perceived experiences. Have you ever known someone who is all about telling you exactly what went on during their day?

A helpful piece of advice is to forgive them for they know not what they do. Even though you do not exactly want to listen to every single specific detail about why everything happened as it happened, you still need to remain present enough for them so that they feel welcome to share their life experiences. You might not know this, but when you feel a lack of patience for someone else, it is simply a pointer that your ego is fighting for survival at that moment, and the lack of patience is a witnessing of selfishness arising in the form of denying the present moment all the while in the company of another person that is doing something that could keep you from doing the same thing. Your ego might want to tell its story, which is how a conversation works. The storyline goes back and forth between opposites, from your story, back to my story. Do you ever notice that when you are talking to someone, you might share first, then their story builds off of your story? Hopefully, you can see the progression that the ego requires mentally to survive here. If you were busy talking about one thing and the other person cut you off and started talking about something completely different, then how do you think your ego would react? Wouldn't you rather go about your day than sit there and listen to a story that means absolutely nothing to you in the present moment? Doesn't your ego value your time more than simply exist in the present moment without the need to change it? Have you ever just stood there and let someone express themselves through a story that was not interesting? These simple silly things might not seem like much, but to the other person, they might seem like the world. This is why it is important to be present for all others. Your ego might not place any significance on the present moment as it is unfolding listening to a meaningless story, but to the other person, it might make or break their day, or even possibly their life.

Imagine the biggest fan of a celebrity in the world finally getting to shake hands with the person they have worshipped mentally for years. What if that fan wanted to tell that celebrity the most important thing that he could think of, and the celebrity wanted nothing to do with it? Imagine how devastated that fan would be if he felt like he had waited his entire life for that moment. When the illusion that is created in the mind crumbles, the opposite of happiness is experienced. The mind can then react and lead a person to suicide for all kinds of reasons that are simply more mental egoic illusions, but at the time they seem so incredibly real that it is almost impossible to distinguish the non-reactive self-awareness that is always present during the super reactive mind-dominated state of consciousness. All suffering is avoidable if only non-reaction was the first thing you were aware of at all times.

This state of being is called full self-awareness and it is the reason enlightened people are always depicted as sitting peacefully. The non-reaction stems from the awareness of the present moment where nothing needs to be changed and it is always accepted as existing perfectly as it is. It is not the reaction to arising thoughts that makes you human, it is the reaction that leaves you stuck being only human. To only be human is to only know suffering. The peace everyone is searching for does not lie in the awareness of your perceived humanity. Peace lies in the awareness of the nothingness of the present moment all the while experiencing your perceived humanity. If you only know one extreme, how are you ever going to be present enough to know that it has an opposite at all times? No matter how tough life gets for you, there is always an opposite available instantly. The only thing that stops you from always experiencing that state of being is your reactive egoic nature. When you are always reacting to life then you are always buying into the storyline of the mind-dominated state of consciousness. That storyline will always have a progression. The ego is kind of like buying a new house. When you are a baby, the house is empty, but as you grow into an adult the house slowly becomes filled with all kinds of things that are collected over the years and labeled valuable. This progression of mental attachments is the source of all human suffering. It is only through the releasement of these mental attachments that true peace is ever experienced. The mind seeks to limit, while consciousness is the only true definition of freedom that there is.

The true depth of spaciousness that is available to your consciousness could not possibly be measured. Your consciousness is so eternal that any situation that arises in the present moment will never be too much to accept. There will always be space to exist in peace even during the most horrific witnessing of the most tragic crimes. The justice system might not agree with your non-reaction during a horrible situation, but witnessing anything arising does not always demand an immediate egoic reaction. Some people end up playing the part of the hero, while others freeze up experiencing severe anxiety. Neither response is right or wrong ultimately, because one response is a reaction to the ego while the other takes on a pure witnessing role. The reactive person usually gets the credit in terrible situations, but sometimes the non-reactive person also deserves some credit. After all, it always seems easier to hurt someone who has already hurt someone else, but to truly end the violence we need to all learn non-reaction over immediately reacting without giving it any thought because no self-awareness is present. It is all an automatic response based on past conditioning.

Chapter 52

SUFFERING AND THE END OF SUFFERING

IN THE EGO EXPERIENCE, suffering is perceived all around us. It is a part of our daily lives as we suffer from small disruptions that seem minuscule to sometimes big or tragic disruptions that almost seem life-ending like you can't go on. The problem with viewing suffering from the mind-dominated state of consciousness is that it is one of the hardest illusions to let go of, because it is happening to every single person on earth in one form or another, every single day of their life. Suffering is so widespread that it seems like it will always be more real than peace and happiness ever will be for humanity. Peace and happiness come and go for some people, but suffering is always there for every single person on earth all the time. Unfortunately, suffering is more readily available than happiness ever will be in the mind-dominated state of consciousness. If you want to suffer, just turn on the television or start calling all of your friends and family and asking them how their day is going. You can pick up any newspaper and practically the entire content of it revolves around suffering. The only way to end suffering is to educate others on living in the present moment. How many people do you know that will tell you that ultimately suffering is an illusion?

How many people do you know that will tell you that there is always an opposite available to you at this very moment and during the moments when suffering hurts the most? I'm rarely sure that you might ever come across someone with the understanding between living in the mind and living in the present moment where all things in the mind are witnessed instead of experienced as complete reality.

Although suffering takes on a different form than happiness, ultimately it is no different. Suffering resides in the individual who witnesses it in the mind and reacts to those thoughts as reality. As with all things contained in the mind, the moment you practice non-reaction is the moment that the reality of the mental concept can be seen as an illusion, because without a reaction where is the proof that it is real? The ego experience requires proof at all times which is why the structure of the ego is deeply rooted in action or reaction. If you wanted to experience sadness then wouldn't you ultimately need to add together sad thoughts, mixed with sad emotions, mixed with a sad attitude toward the present moment and the people around you to attempt to truly create sadness? Those few examples are an inward creation of the ego which wants to experience sadness. The ego will always have an opposite, so an outward creation of sadness requires something like your cat dying or your house burning down or something outwardly happening that allows you to inwardly experience sadness as real. Have you ever asked yourself why sadness is only a reality during those moments when something arises that requires sadness? Why is sadness not witnessed when you are happy? If sadness is absolutely real and eternal, then where does it go? Why is it not experienced twenty-four hours a day seven days a week? This is just another example of the arising and subsiding of the mind-dominated state of consciousness because when a mental form arises, interconnectedness dictates that all of the other little bits and pieces that create the concept also have to arise to help create the illusion. The strength of the illusion depends on how many things are added to the mental concept of what is trying to be created. For example, if your cat died and you experienced deep suffering then you would need to have collected a storyline of love, memories, emotional attachments and photographs, and all kinds of things tied together to form a deep sadness. The moment you begin removing each form from the concept like love and memories and emotional attachments and photographs and all of the interconnected things that made up the love you had for your cat based on past experiences. What do you have left? What reasons are there to suffer so deeply? As each attachment to the past is removed the suffering diminishes.

When someone else's cat dies, do you suffer so deeply? Of course, not because the egoic attachments are not held firmly in mind as they are when it is YOUR cat. This is why it is so important to learn to live your life in the present moment where you no longer carry mental attachments to the past with you that can create the illusion of suffering. If life is lived in the present moment, then enough consciousness is present to understand that everything that arises will eventually subside.

There is enough spaciousness or room for the understanding that the true suffering stems from your inability to live life presently with your cat appreciating every moment you had with that particular form while it was here instead of mourning it after it is gone. So much of life is lived on the mental surface of the ego where you wish you had loved deeper, or you wish had more time with someone to tell them or show them how you felt. Regret is just another pointer that you are not living your life in the present moment.

Hopefully, you can begin to see that true suffering is simply a denial of the present moment no matter what form it takes from being treated wrong, to the loss of a loved one, to violence to all the horrific forms contained in the mind. True suffering stems from all of the negative labels that exist in the mind. The most important thing to understand about suffering is it only happens within every one of us. True suffering is a personal experience that ultimately has nothing to do with what is going on outwardly in the world any more than it has to do with what we witness arising in the mind. True suffering stems from not living in alignment with the present moment. If the majority of your consciousness is heavily stuck in the past or heavily focused on the future, then how do you ever expect to fully be centered in the present? Suffering exists because of not having enough space consciously to be able to see that no matter what is witnessed in the mind there is always an opposite available at the same time. When you can only see one solution to any problem, it is a pointer that the ego experience is dominating your awareness. When you can only see pain and suffering after something bad happens to you then you only know how to live in the mind. When you can see both extremes of the mind being available and existing in the same time and space then that is true self-awareness.

Living presently is having the ability to choose what you want to experience instead of the storyline of your ego choosing for you automatically. As with all things in this world, the choice to end the entire suffering of the world begins with us as an individual. If you choose to live presently and no longer suffer, no matter what arises, then you have taken the first step to ending human suffering. The more people become aware of their consciousness, the more human suffering will begin to diminish globally. Each change that we want to see in the world needs to begin with us alone. There is no point in spending your entire life helping others when you have not helped yourself first to understand what kind of help others truly need. When you become fully self-aware you will no longer try to be another finger plugging another hole in another dam somewhere trying to hold the water back from flooding. You will instead realize that the entire problem was never the flooding, but your egoic viewpoint on flooding was the problem all along. To say that something, like flooding, does not have the right to arise is to say that you have already chosen to suffer. Suffering will always exist for those who fully believe it to be a real thing by not realizing that all things contained in the mind will continue to arise and subside no matter whether you want them to or not. The sooner you work at pushing away your attachment to the world of form, the sooner you will experience less suffering in your life. Learn to accept the world around you as it exists without the egoic need to change it to experience unconditional love and compassion for all who are experiencing it as it was never the world that was the problem, but each of our limited views and mental beliefs that have created it to be what it is today. All of the problems that we have in the world all stem from ego-selfishness. Selfishness and greed dominate the ego experience, and because of it all of humanity is forced to suffer. The few people who are out there in the world trying to make a difference to end suffering are not able to do so because the selfishness of the ego far outweighs the unselfishness of the few.

As an example, this planet produces more than enough food to feed every single person on Earth. Yet people are dying from starvation every single day. The selfishness of the ego dictates that it is not cost-effective to feed people who cannot pay for food. The few people who are giving away free food are only attempting to hold the flood back by plugging another hole in another dam somewhere in the world. I cannot stress enough that you cannot combat the problems of the world solely by outward means alone. The change needs to start on a personal level with me and with you. If we can change, then others can change, and if others can change then eventually the selfish nature of the ego will begin to diminish. Starvation might not end globally overnight, but the sooner it ends in your backyard the sooner it will spread and eventually work itself completely around the world and maybe only then will we ever see a day when not a single person on earth experiences starvation!

Suffering takes on many forms, but each one of those forms is rooted in the ego experience. The sooner we work towards becoming aware of our selfish ways the sooner we can begin to see a difference in our own lives. You have to understand that our own life IS our world. The conceptualized world that exists in the mind is irrelevant and we can do nothing to fix that. Suffering is contagious, and the sooner we no longer suffer, the sooner we don't make others suffer, and the sooner others no longer make people they know suffer, and so on. Try to think about your life as being a virus, what do you want to spread to others today? Hopefully, you will see that suffering starts with you, but more importantly, it can end with you and that is only found by stepping out of the shadow of your ego and living your life in the light of true self-awareness where all things are possible!

Chapter 53

I AM NOTHING

THE EASIEST WAY TO know if you have completely lost yourself in the world of form is to imagine having someone take it all away from you. Everything you have ever worked for, everything that you believe yourself to be, everything that has ever meant anything to you. If someone were to take it all away, what would you be? If the answer is NOTHING, then that alone is a great pointer to the mind-dominated state of consciousness. If you have no awareness of your formless nature, then it shouldn't come as no surprise as to why you suffer so much during the constant changes that life throws your way. If you have no awareness of your consciousness, then it is easily understandable to see why you might cling so tightly to the world of form. The illusion is so strong in your life that if you ever took a single step backward in your life's progression, suffering would arise and possibly even deep suffering. It's no wonder why some people, who just lose one thing of form like their marriage or their job, would go as far as to kill themselves. Without the form held securely in the egoic mind, there is NOTHING left to live for. The ego fights for survival so heavily sometimes that you might end up wanting to kill yourself over the thought that you just can't go on living being a nobody in this world. Your ego might have fought its entire life to be "somebody" to the point that the single thought arising that you might be a "nobody" could very well be too much to take.

Luckily this is an extreme example and most of us fall somewhere between the two extremes, usually experiencing something like depression for as long as it takes to come back to the present moment, and then we move on with our lives to the next thing of form that will arise to take its place.

Sometimes during these extremely difficult times in our lives, it is very helpful to just stop what you are doing and stop all the horrible things you are thinking and just sit down for a moment. Take a few deep breaths, close your eyes, and simply exist in the present moment perfectly as you are without needing anything else of form like someone to talk to. Just breathe in and breathe out and slowly bring your awareness back from the deepest parts of the mind that you might have been witnessing and just LET GO. Stop all mental clinging and watch as the narrow-mindedness of the ego slowly begins to widen. As you navigate the perils of your mind, try to notice how one thought has been added to another thought that was also added to another thought that got you to that place of suffering that you were witnessing. Slowly attempt to remove one thought form as you work your way back to the present moment, then remove another layer of the negative concept till you end up with the original thought that allowed you to go so far away from the present moment. Hold that single thought form firmly in your mind for a moment, and just exist with it without reacting to it like you had previously done which took you deeper into the mind-dominated state of consciousness. As you sit there in silence existing with that one thought that almost made it possible to go as far as to even kill yourself, simply look at the nature of how you can exist with it in perfect peace and stillness all because of non-reaction. In the present non-reactive state, you are in you can witness any thought form arising no matter how horrible it is, and because of this non-reactive state of being you have not lost the peaceful stillness of the present moment. That one horrible thought that earlier caused you great mental agitation is now being witnessed arising yet the moment it is not reacted to; you will have the ability to watch it gently subside at a moment of your choosing. It is this state of being that can only be found in the present moment that makes such an experience possible. The moment you no longer cling to the thought-form in an egoic attempt to make it a reality is the moment it gently subsides.

You must understand that the mind is in a constant state of unrest. Thought forms will constantly arise and subside every moment of every day for your entire life if you are not able to find the true peace that the present moment offers you. The present moment will always be your saving grace or your place of salvation. It will always comfort you in ways that are not possible for you to find in the mind. It is your true nature which is why it feels so amazing when you truly touch the present moment deeply. The present moment is the only place that you will ever be able to strip away all things of form until the only thing you have left is the awareness of your consciousness. It is the ultimate state of a peaceful being as there is no longer an awareness of the body or the awareness of the mind. When you touch the present moment deep enough there is no other way to explain it than to simply say it just IS. There is no ego awareness of a "YOU" or a "SOUL" or a container of any kind. There is only the awareness that "I EXIST," or "I AM."

Since we live in a world of opposites, you need to know that both extremes are always available to you every single second of your entire life. Not once will you ever be forced to react to a thought form no matter how intense the egoic pull to react is experienced. If you are at a place where you have lost everything of form and you feel there is nothing left for you to experience, you are wrong. There is an opposite to that thought form available to you at this exact moment that you are reading this. If you feel like you need to be a "somebody" to exist in this world, you have only witnessed one side of life's coin. The side that you have witnessed your entire life is the side that suffering exists on. If you have only ever known suffering your entire life, don't you think it is time to attempt to find the opposite of that experience before you call it quits? If you honestly have nothing left to lose, then you can easily understand that you have everything to gain by your efforts to want better for yourself. I don't mean better as in you go about adding more form to your life by starting over. I mean better as in you continue to experience your formless nature in the present moment while existing in the world of form. You have already fully figured out that the world of form is suffering and only once you have returned home are you able to plug yourself back into the world of form only this time you are not solely counting on it to define who you are. This is how you truly find inner peace by backing out of the world of form fully by touching the present moment deeply, and then reinserting yourself back into the world of form knowing that you are so much more than can ever be purchased with money or good looks or fame. Even though outwardly you might have nothing, inwardly you have everything! The more diligently you work at living your life in the present moment the less suffering you will experience. The less suffering you experience, the more opportunities you will have to truly be happy. Not the egoic happiness that depends on something of form, but true happiness that depends on absolutely nothing of form because you are already "THAT." You already exist as perfection; it is only when you begin to add form back to the mix does this peace or happiness slowly begins to be covered up again and your awareness of it diminishes. Wisdom is knowing that both extremes exist in the mind at the same time even when the ego is only pulling you to one of them!

Chapter 54

WHY AWARENESS IS NEEDED

THE INFORMATION about the awareness of the ego contained in this book was meant for the spiritual seeker who is deeply invested in finding the true nature of their human experience. If the information contained in this book has somehow added something to you in any way other than the acknowledgment that you have already had your own experiences with becoming aware of the ego experience, then you have missed the point of the information. The things I have written about are simply pointers to the ego experience that is happening to each of us daily usually without any true awareness that it is going on. If you feel you are a better or smarter person for having read this book or it has helped you evolve further on your spiritual path, then you are continuing to add things of form to your ego. If you realize that ultimately nothing was gained or lost by reading this book and the only thing you experienced after reading this information was an awareness that your attention needs to return to the present moment, then you have used this information wisely. The best answer I can give as to the reason why the awareness of the ego is so important is it will help you seek the opposite of it when you realize how out of control you have been your entire life, and in doing so will help you fully return to the present moment where it is the only place you will ever truly find your formless self that exists before anything of form ever has a chance to arise. The opposite of the ego experience leads to the end of all human suffering. The doorway to full self-realization can only be found in this very moment. It is always present even when you are going about your normal daily routines. It is always there even while meditating.

Don't focus on what is arising during meditation. Instead, focus on the fact that something is always arising and subsiding during meditation. The doorway is always open it is just waiting for you to un-focus the attention that you fully place on the ego experience or the world of form. You slowly begin to un-focus the attention you place on the ego by beginning to question why history has to constantly repeat itself in your life. Don't look at the event itself because it always has a slightly different form to it but look at why when suffering arises is there always an immediate attempt to avoid it. Why do you constantly need to react the same way every time to the same situations that constantly arise in your life? Why when someone wrongs you do you feel you need to wrong them somehow in return? Why when someone yells at you do you automatically feel anxiety or negative thoughts and emotions instantly arising? Why are you never able to stop arguing with your significant other until you feel you have won, or someone has walked away from the argument? The why needs to be given awareness as the situations are happening. You don't need to dwell on WHY after the fact as you will just go deeper into the mind. You need to question the argument, as it's happening in the moment to witness a gap in the ego experience. Consciousness needs to be brought into the present moment to push away the continuation of the defensive ego that is simply reacting to the form the argument is taking.

If after an extended number of years on a spiritual search, you are still looking for the next piece of spiritual teaching that is going to take you to the next level, you have already lost yourself in the form of a spiritual search. You would be better off taking one single piece of spiritual insight and giving it your full attention. Keep it in mind twenty-four hours a day, and never let it out of your immediate awareness. No matter what the subject of the teaching is, it will help you learn to remain present. The moment you lose awareness of the teaching you automatically go back away from the present moment and deeper into the flow of the ego experience.

If you are waiting to achieve the next level in meditation for your guru to help you continue to advance to the next level of consciousness, you both are still stuck in the mind-dominated state of consciousness. Anybody that tells you that you are lost or somehow lacking something that only they can give you is not somebody that you need to learn anything from other than to use what they are attempting to do to you as another pointer for you to see another aspect of the ego experience.

Acknowledgments

To my mother, Cheri. I can't say anything other than I love you more than words can express. You have taught me the most about unconditional love for all others regardless of their circumstances. Your compassion knows no bounds and is a steady anchor for all of the people around you. You have always pushed tradition on us and kept the best parts of family alive! It's been such a blessing to have you there during some of the most painful times of my life. I appreciate all of the time we have been able to spend together over the past several years and all of the encouragement and support through the good times and the bad.

I also want to thank my dad, Tim. We have had so much fun together growing up and I will never forget that! You have always been the Zen Master in my life! You never overreact when negative things happen, and I love that about you! Every problem has a solution in your world, and you always strive to create a beautiful life! You are the best father I could have ever asked for!

To my stepfather, Steve. You are so patient and so kind to everybody around you. We've never had an argument, and you have been such a good role model. I have drawn lots of inspiration from watching how well you treat not only my mother all of these years but also the rest of us kids and grandkids. You will always have my love and respect, and I will always enjoy your company!

To my publishing coach, Stacey. Thank you so much for being so patient with me and being so professional and teaching me the steps to publishing my book! I'm positive every person you have helped through this process is as grateful as I am. I hope to work with you again in the future!

Thank you, Jeff. You have pushed me to finish my book, put me in touch with Stacey, and been the champion in my life to be a better person! You have always been a brother from another mother! We have been lifelong friends and I have always looked up to you and enjoyed your success in life! I love you, brother!

To Jake, we have been through so much together over the years! I love you and all of your kids like my own. We always strive to do better when we are together, and I love that about our friendship! You never give up and I see nothing but success in your future! You have been and always will be family to me!

Kosol. Thank you so much for teaching me Stargating and how to shift my consciousness. You have shown me what a multi-dimensional existence looks like and I never would have seen past the illusion of the ego experience without you!

Thank you, Heideh for playing a significant part in helping me expose my own ego and my attachment to it. You worked through the hardest experiences of your life and came out on top. I'm so proud of you! Slinky and Dharma will love you forever!

Dan, you have been another one of my best friends since I've known you. We both share the same daily experiences and you have always overcome more than I have. Your compassion and generosity never go unnoticed over the years and I always appreciate your encouragement daily! You always set the pace and lead the way!

Thank you, Aliesha for being a wonderful and positive friend to me daily, for being my book's first beta reader, and for giving me all your useful feedback to help me improve it! We have always helped keep each other present when the ego starts to take over from the emotional/mental/physical struggles of daily life. You always shine bright like a diamond. You help guide everybody to overcome their struggles and deliver them back to a positive place! Your unconditional love and happy disposition never go unnoticed, which is why everybody is drawn to you like a moth to a flame. Always remain grateful for the lessons and struggles you have had to overcome in your life (and have yet to overcome), and you will never lose that beautiful light that shines so brightly in you!

Finally, I would like to thank all of my readers! I hope this book serves as a guide on your journey to self-discovery. It is only when you begin questioning everything that you slowly start peeling back all the layers of the ego. When there is nothing left and the need for familiar suffering has subsided, you can then begin building back a life that you want to experience in the present moment. I wish everybody the best of luck and always remember to be the change you seek in the world!

About the Author

Tim has been a Usui Shiki Ryoho Reiki Master and Stargate Meditation practitioner for nineteen years. After traditional medicine failed him, he embarked on a transformative journey into the realms of energy healing and consciousness shifting, which ultimately led him to seek the root of his consciousness and the unraveling of the nature of the ego in order to  understand human suffering. It has been through his own suffering that the self-awareness behind this book was born. Tim offers this book as a small glimpse into the nature of the human ego and the suffering that arises from it, but more importantly how it is possible to end that suffering.

* 9 7 9 8 9 8 9 3 1 0 2 0 3 *